Indian
by Choice

Text © Amit Dasgupta 2009
Art © Wisdom Tree
Photographs – Title page - Ranjit Oberoi, Page 42, 43 - Dinodia Photo Library pvt. ltd.

First published 2009

ISBN HB 978-81-8328-136-2
     PB 978-81-8328-140-9

Published by
Wisdom Tree,
4779/23, Ansari Road,
Darya Ganj, New Delhi-2
Ph.: 23247966/67/68
wisdomtree@vsnl.com

Printed in India at Print Perfect

Indian
by Choice

Amit Dasgupta
Art : Neelabh

wisdom
tree

Mandy is a second generation Indian, born and brought up in Chicago. He is as American as they come — hot dogs, French fries, baseball and the love of all things American, especially blonde. He is, of course, no different from his clones who are in several other parts of the world — England and Australia, the Netherlands and Canada. They blend with their surroundings by assimilating the culture of their adopted home and denying their Indian roots and heritage. In the case of the hero of our book, he has even changed his name from Mandeep to Mandy!

The story begins with a wedding in the family back home in India. Weddings, in India, are a major event for all family members — both near and distant — to get together. Mandy's parents are, unfortunately, unable to go to India as Mandy's mum has just had an accident. So the mantle falls on Mandy, who naturally hates the thought of visiting India. But he has little choice in the matter and reluctantly boards the flight with an excursion ticket, which he ensures will get him back to Chicago in four weeks time. Now, read on.....

ji - a sign of respect; *Suniye* - listen; *Behenji* - sister; *khane mein kya hai?* - what food are you serving today?; *Bilkulji* - for sure

Whenever you see, Mummy this and Mummy that. My family same thing.
I am *toh* fed up. But, what I am to do. Lady wife is always telling,
Arrey they are *bachhas*, no? All life *bachhas!*

But Indians are quite different in Chicago, aren't they? They behave so American.

Yes, yes, but this is Indian Air and it is going to *Bharat Mata. Bus.* What to say. Here we are *khulla khulla.* We are Indians. *Amricanism* is for Chicago immigration when we return!

Haath milao partner!

Hi, I am Mandy and I live in Chicago.

Mandy? *Arrey dost, Mandeep kaho na,* ya Maninder. What is this Mandy nonsense?

bachhas - kids; *Bharat Mata* - Mother India; *khulla khulla* - open about things; *Haath milao partner* - shake hands; *kaho* - say

Sometime later, anxiety gives in to fatigue...

Attention please...ladies and gentlemen.

We are getting ready to land at the Indira Gandhi International Airport; please keep your seat belts fastened. The current temperature in New Delhi is eight degrees Centigrade and the local time is 3.45 am. We enjoyed having you on board and look forward to welcoming you again. Namaste.

Oye - hi; *O paji* - brother; *gale lag yaar* - give me a hug buddy; *bhai* - brother

Uncle aa gaye...
Uncle aa gaye!!

Listen ji,
Mandeep beta has come.

aa gaye – has come; beta - son

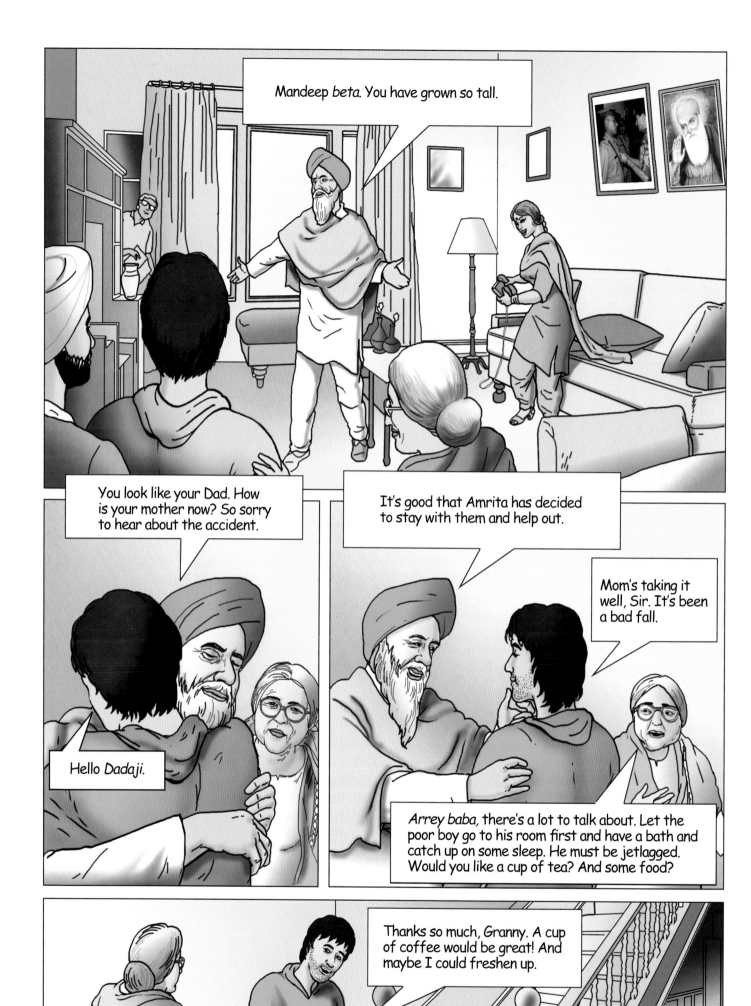

Gurinder shows Mandy his room...

Used to be my room but I've moved upstairs. I still use it sometimes to watch TV or listen to music.

Wondering who they are?? Cricketers! we are all cricket fans, or should I say fanatics!

Cricket?? Don't know the game.

Gurinder smiles and leaves him to rest. Mandy can't control his urge to write to his parents...

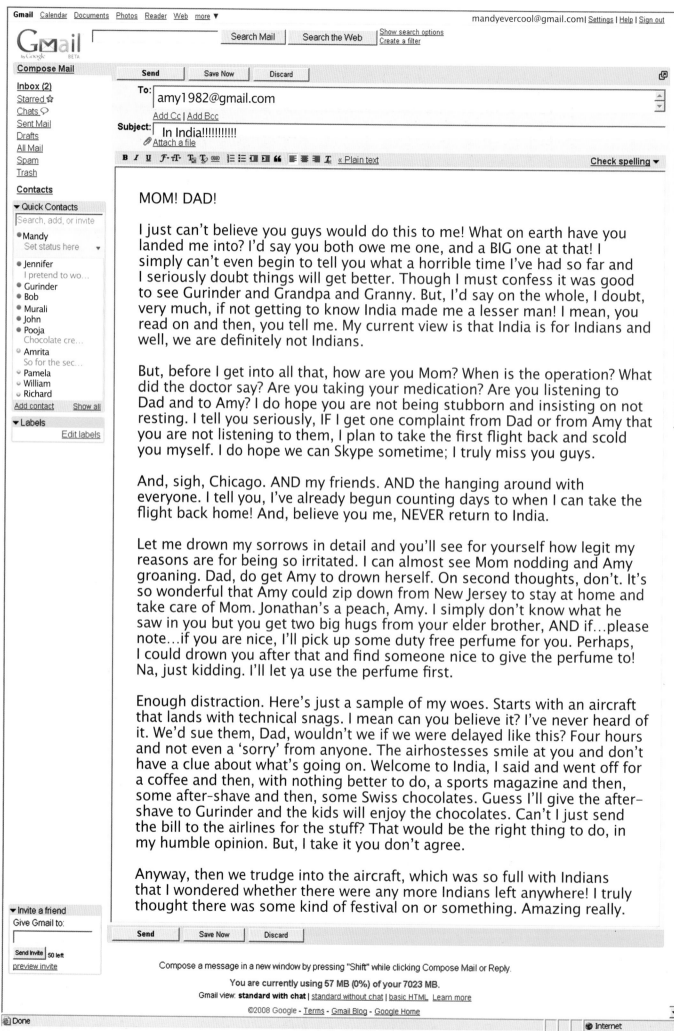

Gmail
by Google BETA

Search Mail   Search the Web   Show search options
Create a filter

Compose Mail   Send   Save Now   Discard

Inbox (2)   To: amy1982@gmail.com
Starred ☆
Chats ◯   Add Cc | Add Bcc
Sent Mail   Subject: In India!!!!!!!!!!!
Drafts   Attach a file
All Mail
Spam   B I U 𝓕·𝓣· 𝐓ₐ𝐓ₓ ∞ ≣ ≣ ⫤ ⫣ 66 ≣ ≣ ⫥ 𝐼 « Plain text   Check spelling ▼
Trash

Contacts

▼ Quick Contacts

Search, add, or invite

● Mandy
  Set status here   ▼

● Jennifer
  I pretend to wo...
● Gurinder
● Bob
● Murali
● John
● Pooja
  Chocolate cre...
◉ Amrita
  So for the sec...
● Pamela
◉ William
◉ Richard

Add contact   Show all

▼ Labels
  Edit labels

MOM! DAD!

I just can't believe you guys would do this to me! What on earth have you landed me into? I'd say you both owe me one, and a BIG one at that! I simply can't even begin to tell you what a horrible time I've had so far and I seriously doubt things will get better. Though I must confess it was good to see Gurinder and Grandpa and Granny. But, I'd say on the whole, I doubt, very much, if not getting to know India made me a lesser man! I mean, you read on and then, you tell me. My current view is that India is for Indians and well, we are definitely not Indians.

But, before I get into all that, how are you Mom? When is the operation? What did the doctor say? Are you taking your medication? Are you listening to Dad and to Amy? I do hope you are not being stubborn and insisting on not resting. I tell you seriously, IF I get one complaint from Dad or from Amy that you are not listening to them, I plan to take the first flight back and scold you myself. I do hope we can Skype sometime; I truly miss you guys.

And, sigh, Chicago. AND my friends. AND the hanging around with everyone. I tell you, I've already begun counting days to when I can take the flight back home! And, believe you me, NEVER return to India.

Let me drown my sorrows in detail and you'll see for yourself how legit my reasons are for being so irritated. I can almost see Mom nodding and Amy groaning. Dad, do get Amy to drown herself. On second thoughts, don't. It's so wonderful that Amy could zip down from New Jersey to stay at home and take care of Mom. Jonathan's a peach, Amy. I simply don't know what he saw in you but you get two big hugs from your elder brother, AND if...please note...if you are nice, I'll pick up some duty free perfume for you. Perhaps, I could drown you after that and find someone nice to give the perfume to! Na, just kidding. I'll let ya use the perfume first.

Enough distraction. Here's just a sample of my woes. Starts with an aircraft that lands with technical snags. I mean can you believe it? I've never heard of it. We'd sue them, Dad, wouldn't we if we were delayed like this? Four hours and not even a 'sorry' from anyone. The airhostesses smile at you and don't have a clue about what's going on. Welcome to India, I said and went off for a coffee and then, with nothing better to do, a sports magazine and then, some after-shave and then, some Swiss chocolates. Guess I'll give the after-shave to Gurinder and the kids will enjoy the chocolates. Can't I just send the bill to the airlines for the stuff? That would be the right thing to do, in my humble opinion. But, I take it you don't agree.

Anyway, then we trudge into the aircraft, which was so full with Indians that I wondered whether there were any more Indians left anywhere! I truly thought there was some kind of festival on or something. Amazing really.

▼ Invite a friend
Give Gmail to:

Send Invite | 50 left
preview invite

Send   Save Now   Discard

Compose a message in a new window by pressing "Shift" while clicking Compose Mail or Reply.

You are currently using 57 MB (0%) of your 7023 MB.

Gmail view: **standard with chat** | standard without chat | basic HTML Learn more

©2008 Google - Terms - Gmail Blog - Google Home

Done   Internet

A handful of foreigners were thrown in, by which I mean they did not belong to India or were not Indians by origin. First class, Business and Economy were all full!

Most of the passengers on the aircraft were Indians either with US passports or long-term residents. They were shocking in their behaviour. I saw a swift transformation in their behaviour that I would never have believed! While they hung around at O'Hare and I saw quite a few of them at the coffee shop and then, at Immigration, they were polite and quiet and well, quite American. They get on to the aircraft and they are… like from outer space or some such. I read in a paper that Indians like to spit a lot and urinate in public. Well, they didn't do that in the aircraft. Thank God! But, believe me, they truly misbehaved. They were garrulous and loud and inconsiderate and ill-dressed and well, let me put it this way, I felt so ashamed of these guys. I mean they are US citizens after all.

The airhostesses tried their best to calm them down. I compliment them for their patience and their tolerance. My fear is that they sort of expected this kind of behaviour from the passengers, which is possibly why most of the airhostesses looked so matronly. I almost called one of them *Maaji*. No Ma, do relax, I didn't even utter the word. At least, not loudly. And no Amy, there were no pretty airhostesses on the aircraft and I have not invited anyone to dinner. If you only saw them! Ugh!

I need to tell you about the husband and wife sitting beside me. Perfect dumbbells, as Dad would say. Spouting (or is it, sprouting?) gems from every finger. Wife with gold necklaces that had her stooping all the time. And such colourful taste in clothes! Would put a rainbow to shame! And the guy justified the misbehaviour of the Indians almost giving the impression that it was their right to behave like that on an Indian carrier! Truly Mom, how do we produce such jerks?

But, the real problem is that both he and then, the Immigration officer at Delhi airport had the cheek to make fun of my name. They kept asking me what this 'Mandy' was and insisted that I must be Mandeep or Maninder or whatever. What's up, Dad? I don't understand this and I found it very disturbing. I don't like being called Mandeep. I gave it up years ago. I don't feel like a Mandeep, if you know what I mean. In as much as I don't see Amrita as anything but Amy. Can you ever think our neighbour Jackson would respond to Jaikishen? Why is it so difficult to understand? Why do Indian Indians insist that I have to be what I simply am not. My identity is American and I am accepted in the US as Mandy by all my friends. Even by the bank and the credit card companies, and the American passport issuing authority. So, that is who I am. What's with all this Mandeep business? And why should a perfect stranger insist on quizzing me on this?

You told me, Dad, that Indians ask a lot of questions. I can accept that. But where personal matters are concerned, they should stay away. I don't ask them why their wife looks so terrible in what she wears. Do I? Or, is it that I should? Just to square things a bit, if you know what I mean. I could say, "I'll tell you more about why I am Mandy and not Mandeep if you tell me why you and your wife look, dress, talk and behave like such perfect idiots?" Do give me your advice on this and make it *jaldi*.

Landing into Delhi was another thing I need to tell you guys. Some dots appeared in an otherwise black landscape, which I presume were lights and not the night sky up side down! It was all as exciting as walking into a dark room with sunglasses! I was truly disappointed. Just imagine landing into Chicago or New York or even Paris or London or Sydney. It's such a pleasure. You capture the city at one wonderful stroke and everything inside you tells you, it's going to be a wonderful experience. The sheer darkness as you enter Delhi tells you there is a mystery outside and it is simply not inviting. Sort of scares you. Quite frankly, I rate it as a bad experience.

Yet, there were others in the aircraft that appeared quite excited as the aircraft made its descent. Many clapped and someone actually said, "*Bharat Mata ki jai!*" I quite frankly don't think I will understand this! I mean IF this means being Indian, well, quite frankly I don't think I am cut out to being one. I don't feel like one. I don't behave like one. And, going by the behaviour of those in the aircraft, I don't think I'll ever like to behave like anyone of them. They can keep their India and their Indianness, thank you very much.

Immigration and Customs were no problem apart from the fact that the immigration officer tried to act funny with my name. That apart, it was so wonderful to see Gurinder and such a large gang of relatives. Soono and Ranee and Tonto and...well, I've forgotten their names. I was truly touched. It was around four o'clock in the morning and the kids and others had all come to pick me up.

The drive down was the most depressing thing ever. You need to be blind if you have to visit India. The poverty hits you; the number of people hit you. Of course, Mom, I know there are poor in America and we have seen them in Chicago and in New York, but not in the numbers that I saw here. Out in the streets. On a cold winter morning. Children and women sleeping alongside dogs and without a covering. It is so terribly depressing.

Well, what can I say? I truly do not know what you wanted for me from this experience. As of now, it has been upsetting and horrifying and I quite frankly, want to come home. But Gurinder is getting married tomorrow. Tonight there is the *sangeet* and then, tomorrow morning the *shaadi* and in the evening the reception. Frankly, all this ought to be fun because these guys are cool. I've never met Gurinder before, just chatted with him on MSN and we've exchanged e-mails and photos. But the guy is really nice. I've yet to meet Amarjit Uncle and Kulvinder Aunty. They've gone out of town for some last minute shopping. Will go down in a bit and see everyone. By the way, Granny and Grandpa are really nice! They have such kind eyes. Just like yours.

Also, Mom, did I tell you that this house is like a mad house? There's sooooo much activity going on! Everyone is just running around eating or serving *laddoo*s and God alone knows what else! Smells yummy! Don't mind me if I put on pounds by the time I get back!

Love you Mom. Love you Dad. Love you Sis

Mandy

PS: Will write to you regularly. Amy please teach Dad to use the computer! I want a mail from you guys EVERY single day and it should begin with details on how Mom is and how Dad is doing and how you are coping. By the way, Amy, my room needs cleaning. Can ya see to it? Love ya lots. Loads. Squishy hugs.

After a couple of hours of rest, Mandy goes down to meet everyone...

Listen everyone!
Here's Mandy, my handsome cousin from U. S. of A. And Mandy, meet my lovely aunt Nimmo and her son Arvind, and this is...

Hi...

Hello...

Namaste...

Hi...

Yo...

Now, Meet my Daddy*ji* and Mummy*ji*.

Hello. Thank you for having me over.

Later...

I have to pick up a few things. Want to come along?

Would love to!

Lajpat Nagar market...

Jyoti loves South Indian food. I need to find *khara bhaat* mix, *Upma* mix and such like. All MTR. There's a shop here that has all that kind of stuff.

What on earth is *khara bhaat*? I've heard of *dosas* and *idlis* but never tried them.

OK, let's get some education done after we are done with shopping. There's the store for the mix.

Yanna Saar, Namaskaram. Vat time wedding tomorrow? Jyoti madam telephoning and telling me you is coming and I am keeping ready all the mix stuff.

I am putting some *haalmaddi agarbatti* from my side, auspicious occasion no! Rs 200 for mix.

Come early *Rangaji*. We plan to leave the house around ten o'clock.

Well, that's done. Now for that education that I promised you. Let's have some good South Indian coffee.

Well...let's hope I survive it!

16
khara bhaat mix - Indian spices; *Yanna Saar, Namaskaram* - hello sir, greetings; *agarbatti* - incense stick

Defence Colony market offers delicious South Indian food.

Masala dosa and a coffee for me.

They don't serve beer here... in that case, I'll take the same. Now, you tell me about Jyoti. How many years have you known her? You never wrote about her in your e-mails. You wicked sod!

Actually, I don't know her that well. I know enough about her to want to get married to her.

What do you mean? You love her, don't you? And she is not ten years old? I mean this is not a child marriage?

I've met her. Love her? Well, love grows. It takes time. My parents know her parents and both think, we would be a good match. I met her a couple of times and liked her. And she agreed. So, that's that. We'll have many years to discover one another. Sometime during that period, we will fall in love.

What? You'll fall in love after you guys get married? I mean buddy, take a step back and think about what you are saying.

I know what I am saying. Arranged marriages have as much chance of success or indeed, failure, as love marriages. The families think we are perfect. Jyoti and I have met and we think we can give it a go.

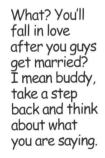

So you get married to a perfect stranger? Is that what love is all about?

I don't know about love but I am marrying someone I believe that my family trusts I will be able to spend my life with, and that we will make each other happy. Look at *Dadaji* and *Dadiji*, or even my parents or for that matter, your parents. Aren't they happy? They all had arranged marriages. Anyways let's go home now before they report us to the Missing Person's Squad.

Mandy checks if there is an e-mail from his sister. He finds a brief message...

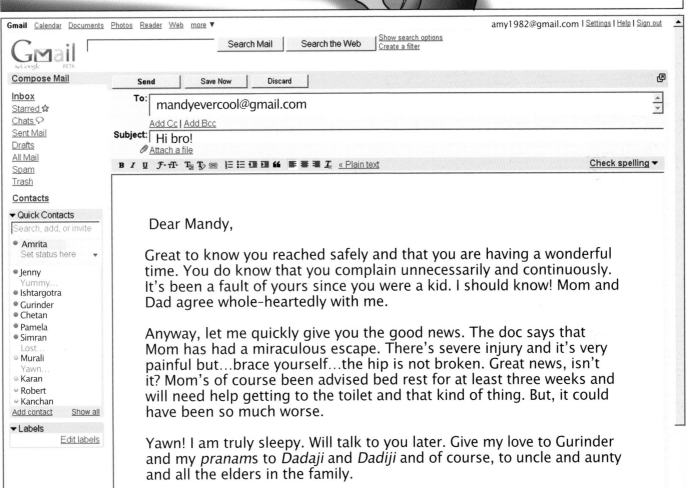

Gmail BETA

Search Mail   Search the Web   Show search options / Create a filter

Compose Mail

Send   Save Now   Discard

To: mandyevercool@gmail.com

Add Cc | Add Bcc

Subject: Hi bro!

Attach a file

B *I* U   𝓕·𝓣· T₂ T₂ ∞   ≔ ≔ ≔ ≔ ⁶⁶   ≡ ≡ ≡ 𝓘   « Plain text   Check spelling ▼

Inbox
Starred ☆
Chats ○
Sent Mail
Drafts
All Mail
Spam
Trash

Contacts

▼ Quick Contacts
Search, add, or invite
● Amrita
Set status here   ▼
● Jenny
Yummy...
● Ishtargotra
● Gurinder
● Chetan
● Pamela
● Simran
Lost...
● Murali
Yawn...
● Karan
● Robert
● Kanchan
Add contact   Show all

▼ Labels
Edit labels

   Dear Mandy,

   Great to know you reached safely and that you are having a wonderful
   time. You do know that you complain unnecessarily and continuously.
   It's been a fault of yours since you were a kid. I should know! Mom and
   Dad agree whole-heartedly with me.

   Anyway, let me quickly give you the good news. The doc says that
   Mom has had a miraculous escape. There's severe injury and it's very
   painful but...brace yourself...the hip is not broken. Great news, isn't
   it? Mom's of course been advised bed rest for at least three weeks and
   will need help getting to the toilet and that kind of thing. But, it could
   have been so much worse.

   Yawn! I am truly sleepy. Will talk to you later. Give my love to Gurinder
   and my *pranam*s to *Dadaji* and *Dadiji* and of course, to uncle and aunty
   and all the elders in the family.

   Big hug to you...and don't you dare forget the perfume!

   Love
   Amrita

pranams - to bow, to greet with respect

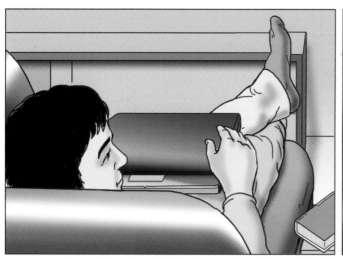

It is the tallest brick minaret in the world and is an important example of Indo-Islamic architecture. Listed as a UNESCO World Heritage Site, it is 72.5 metres high.

It's evening and Mandy is all dressed up for the *sangeet*...

Namaste Dadaji!

My American grandson! Wow! You look like an Indian prince from America!

Your *Dadiji* bought the right *achkan* for you. You look like a *sona munda* in this, and it has fitted you well. Keep counting how many lovely girls will fall for you! Ha ha ha!...

I heard from Amy, *Dadaji*. The doc says, Mom hasn't broken her hip but has suffered severe injury. Needs to have bed rest for around three weeks or so. Amy and everyone at home send their love.

That's really good news. Let's raise a toast to that.

Mandy gets a drink and then moves off to greet other guests...

He joins a group of young people...

I am Mandy. Gurinder's cousin.

Mandy is Mandeep, *nahi?*

No. It's **Mandy** for **Mandy.**

Arrey this *Amricanism* gets me! I am Sandeep. So I am Sandy? And that is Joginder and so he is Jogs?

Might do him some good if he jogs.

Arrey yaar, eat, drink and be merry.

I second that.

Dadiji - Grandmother; *achkan* - a traditional Indian long jacket; *sona munda* - handsome boy; *nahi?* - is'nt it?; *yaar* - friend

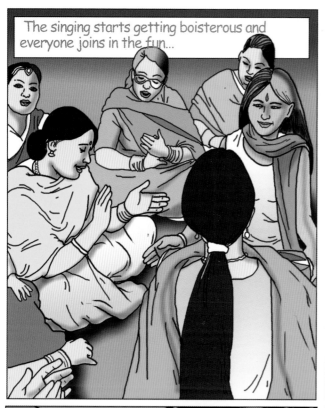

The singing starts getting boisterous and everyone joins in the fun...

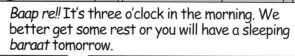

Baap re!! It's three o'clock in the morning. We better get some rest or you will have a sleeping *baraat* tomorrow.

Exhausted, Mandy hits the sack and is out like a light...

Knock!! Knock!!

Gurinder greets him with a set of *kurta pyjama* to wear...

Get up chum. It's 6am. Time to get ready! We do a quick visit to the gurudwara.

Baap re - oh my god; *baraat* - a marriage procession

BANGLA SAHEB GURUDWARA

After offering their prayers, Gurinder and the family come back to get ready for the *baraat*...

Do me a favour son, don't fall off the horse. The family's prestige is at stake.

Ha Ha! Will try not to, *Dadaji*.

The bridegroom is received warmly by the people and the wedding proceedings begin...

Time for the marraige portrait...

Look into the camera please. Smile!

Here...here... Lift your chin a bit please. This is a lifetime memorable moment...

Say cheese!! Smile Gurinder, perhaps your last chance.

It's reception party in the evening...

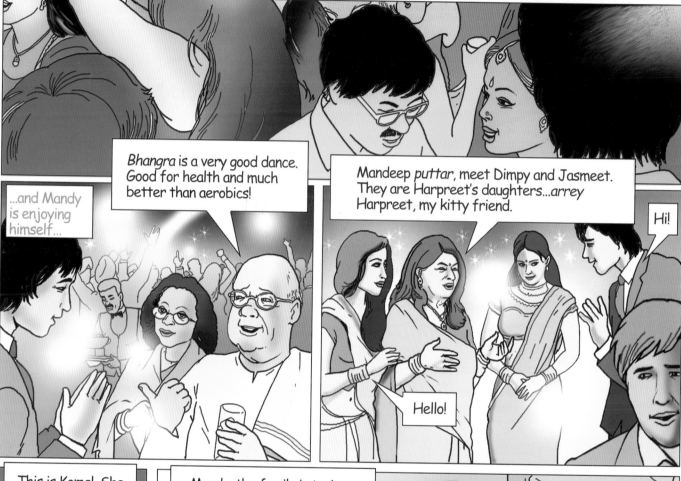

Bhangra is a very good dance. Good for health and much better than aerobics!

...and Mandy is enjoying himself...

Mandeep *puttar*, meet Dimpy and Jasmeet. They are Harpreet's daughters...*arrey* Harpreet, my kitty friend.

Hi!

Hello!

This is Komal. She is doing a Fashion Designing course in Chandigarh.

Hi....

Mandy, the family is trying to get you hitched yaar.

Tell them, we are also eligible and in the queue!

Whaatt!!!

Bhangra - a popular folk dance of Punjab; puttar - son

Though the leg pulling was well intentioned, Mandy is shocked. He slumps through sheer exhaustion on a chair with a drink...

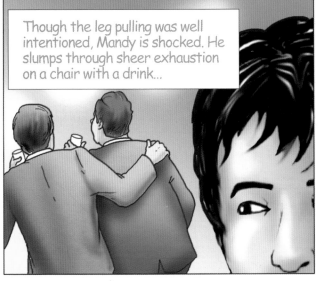

Did Jogs and Sandy really mean that? Are people really trying to fix me up?

That was fun!

Yes it was.

Hi, you must be Mandy. I heard you are from Chicago and this is your first visit to India.

Now! Now!! How do you know my name?

Dadaji told me about you. You probably don't know but he's my grandfather and you and I are cousins. Long lost cousins! And they call me Simrita.

That's great! Now no one will think I am trying to get hitched to you...err...I didn't mean it the way it sounded. It's something Sandeep and Joginder said. Sort of bothered me.

Don't worry about me. I am already spoken for and...by the way, I am so relieved to hear that your mother is not as seriously unwell as everyone thought. We all prayed for her early recovery. Do convey my *pronams* to her when you write to her next.

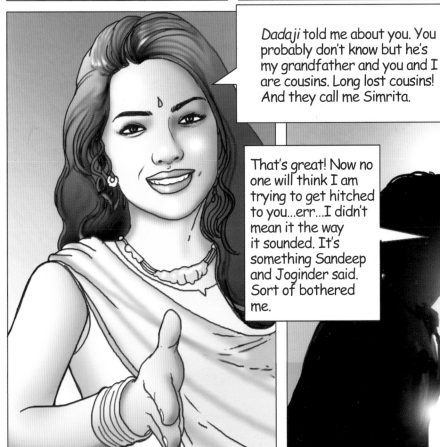

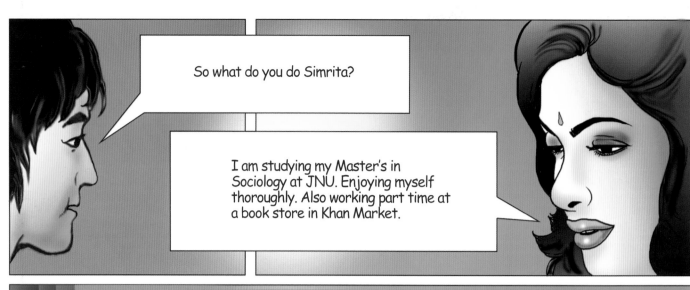

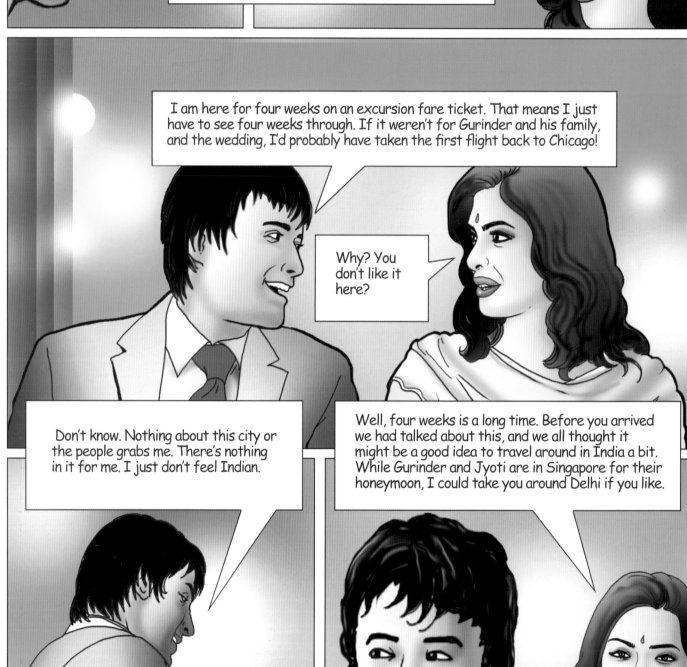

If that's okay with you, I am game.

Good. That's settled then. We can leave after breakfast tomorrow.

Where do I pick you up from?

The dining room! We can leave after breakfast. Didn't I tell you that I live in *Dadaji's* house? He's my grandfather.

Next morning, Mandy is ready to go out for Delhi sightseeing...

Where are you planning to eat your lunch? Drink only bottled water *beta*.

Well, we'll see how brave this American kid is.

Give my best to the love birds and tell them, I'll see them when they get back from Singapore...

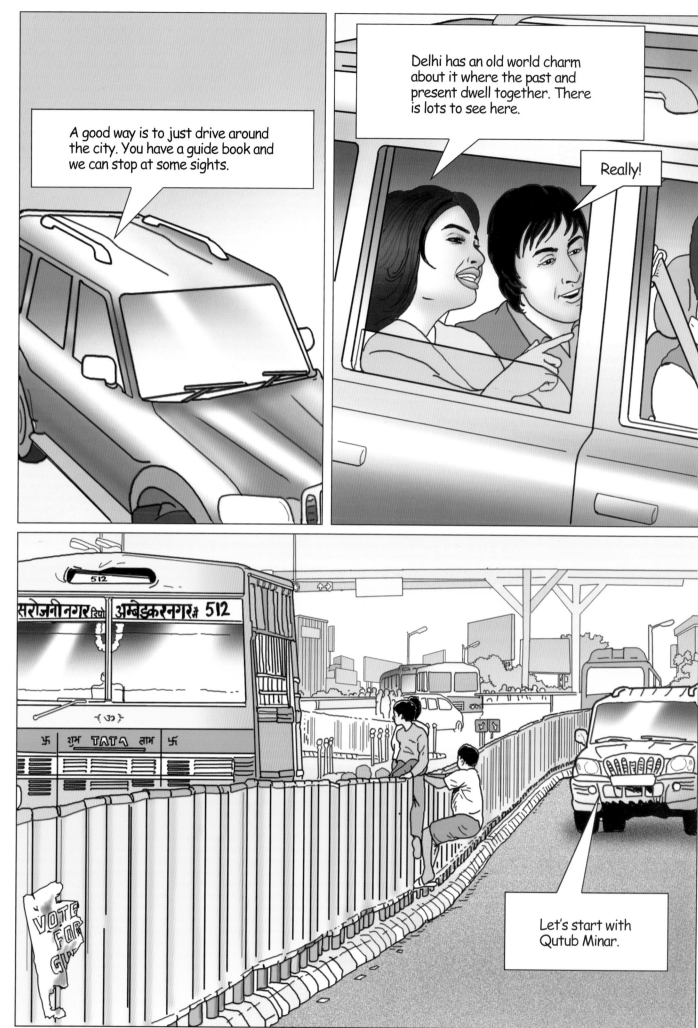

Mandy and Simrita spend the day visiting all the historical places in Delhi. Mandy is busy clicking away with his camera...

QUTUB MINAR

HUMAYUN'S TOMB

I am fascinated by the architecture and elaborate carvings on these monuments Simmi. So much time and dedication must have gone into building them.

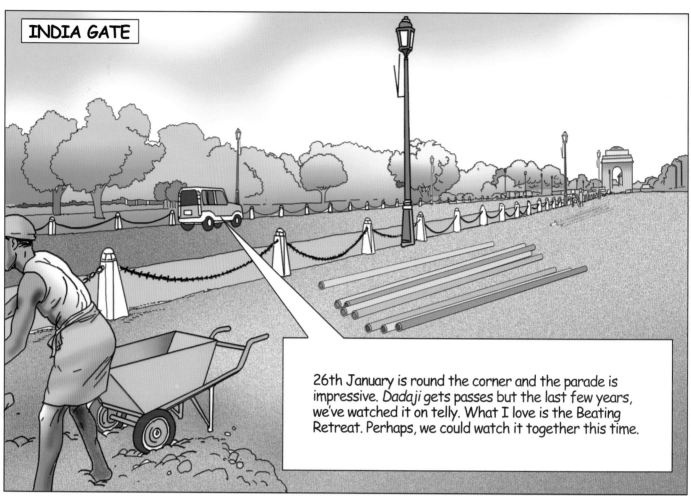

INDIA GATE

26th January is round the corner and the parade is impressive. *Dadaji* gets passes but the last few years, we've watched it on telly. What I love is the Beating Retreat. Perhaps, we could watch it together this time.

PURANA QUILA

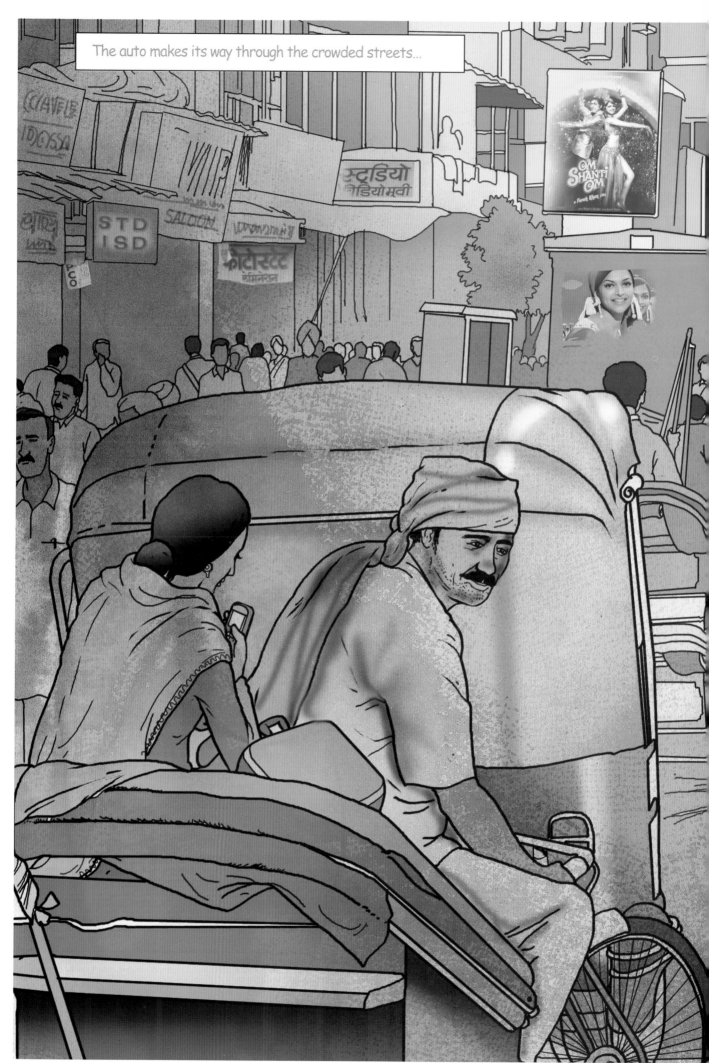

The auto makes its way through the crowded streets...

Established in 1650 AD, this was once the grandest market in India and is the oldest and busiest place in the walled city of Old Delhi. As you can see, it still retains its historical character. Earlier a canal ran through the middle of the street as a part of the water supply scheme. The moonlight reflecting on the water in the canal earned this place its name, *Chandni Chowk* or the 'Moonlight Square'.

You bet, with so many people around, the moonlight doesn't manage to reach the square anymore!

parantha - a kind of Indian bread

It's time to return home...It's traffic time in Delhi...

Now we are crossing Rajghat, which is Gandhi *ji*'s final resting place. I know you would like to go there, but not right now...

It's only *Dadaji* who takes people there. Ask him. He's very touchy. He'll come with you, if he feels you are worth it! Let's stop for some coffee now.

COFFEE BAR

So, what was your first impression?

The past, the history, is interesting. I don't quite like the present.

Like what?

It's the sheer numbers. I hate it. Crawling like flies. They are always here and there. And the poverty. It's there in your face. Beggars and the destitute. I am not used to it.

And there are no poor people in Chicago?

Of course there are. But the poverty, the acuteness of destitution is not like in here!

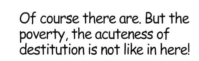

So what did you like about the places you visited?

Delhi is a city of tombs. Of dead people, whom everyone has forgotten. Who remembers Safdarjung? Have you asked the people whom you meet in the streets whether they have heard about Lodhi or Humayun? Betchya, all they will remember is their tombs. Is this what Delhi or India is all about? Thank you, I don't want it. I came here as a tourist and as a tourist, India is great. But, as an Indian born American, I AM SORRY: the place simply does not grab me in any way. It's not my style.

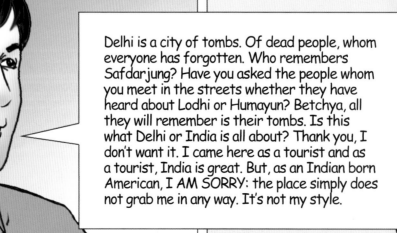

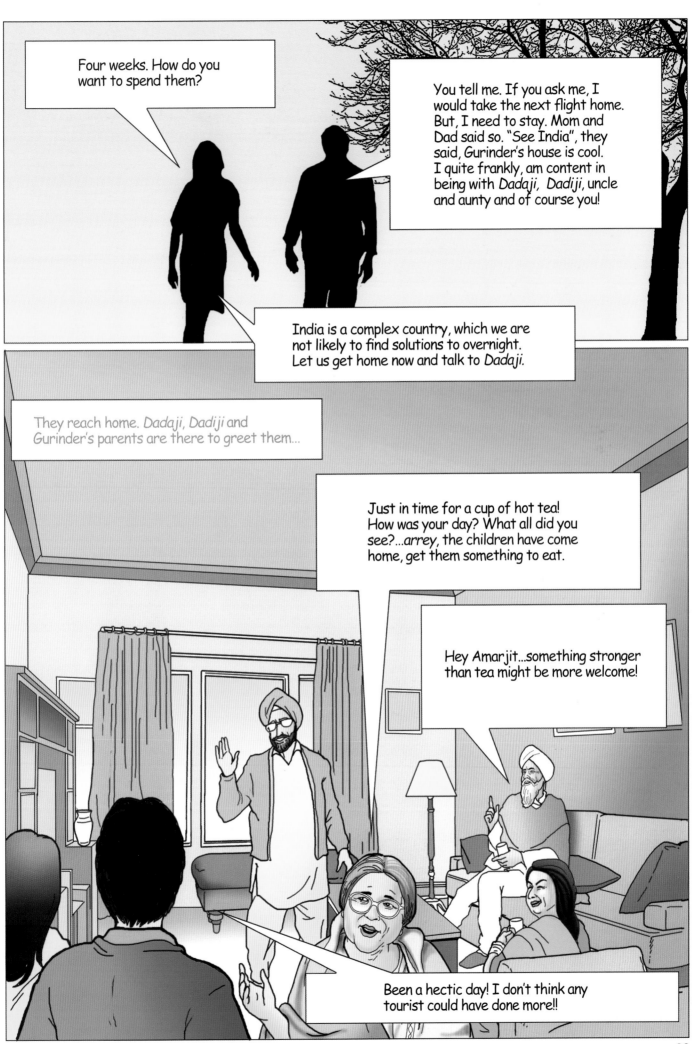

We did most of the sights and even managed Purana Quila and ate at *Paranthewali Gali*. Quite a sport, this American born *desi*.

Well, here are the snacks... *garmagaram* samosas and *namkeen*. I will leave it to your *Dadaji* to take care of what you should drink.

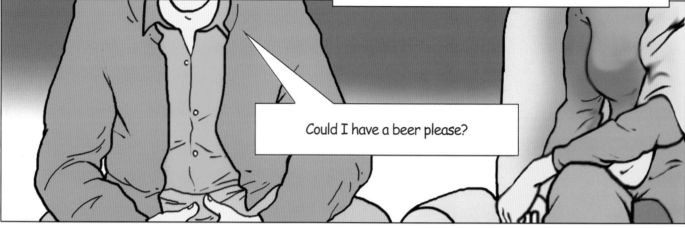

Could I have a beer please?

Mandy is confused about India *Dadaji*. I told him that if he were to talk to you, he would have answers to all his questions.

Haven't quite understood India, *Dadaji*. It is such a complicated place and I really don't have the time or the inclination to figure it all out. I am here for a holiday. Just a holiday. This is not a research or data collection trip. Wanted to be here for Gurinder's wedding and bond with the family. India is just incidental to the whole trip...

garmagaram - piping hot; namkeen - salted Indian snack

But then again, Mom's gone and made sure that I am stuck here for four weeks. She wanted me to travel around and get to know India. Dad said something about roots. But quite frankly, this place is alien to me. Everything about it is different compared to what I am used to or what I am familiar with. There is nothing, absolutely nothing, that I can say attracts me to this place. Apart from all of you.

Phew! And that wasn't even rehearsed!

And you are quite right to feel that way Mandeep. At first sight, India can overwhelm. Even intimidate. There's something about India that prevents you from being indifferent to it. She draws you into taking a position. Either you like her or you don't. But you can't simply walk away as if you are untouched.

What is it about India that you like *Dadaji*?

I can't quite put my finger on it. Maybe it is our ancient history and our culture. Maybe it is the sheer diversity of the country: East to West, North to South, there is so much variety and it seeps into every aspect of daily life — customs, cuisine, clothes, language, music, even the gods we worship vary from place to place.

I like the colours of India; Rajasthan with the desert and all the bright reds and greens and yellows, the East with its lush green, the South with the coolness of water and the colour of flowers, the West with moisture in the air and the smell of the earth. I used to love it when your *Dadaji* would get transferred from one place to another! I would get to see a new place and the very thought excited me!

When I was small and accompanied Papa*ji* to different places, it was a great adventure. What I didn't like was not having permanent friends. Every time we shifted, I had to start all over again. We never stayed anywhere for more than three to four years.

Amarjit and I got married quite a while back and we would visit Papa*ji* and *Maaji* often. It was such fun. And as *Maaji* says, India's diversity is so incredible.

Visual natural beauty is everywhere *Dadaji*. The US has some of the most breathtaking sights.

No one disputes that. I think Nature has been kind and generous to everyone. But I find the beauty in my country something unique. Everytime I visit the desert or the sea or the mountains, I come back having seen something new. I am quite sure, it is the same with every other country in the world and I must confess the Grand Canyon has always been one of my favourite never-seen places.

One cannot live by Nature alone, *Dadaji*. There's so much about India that is awful. The poverty, the dirt, the number of people you see on the streets, you open the newspapers and all you read about is crime and murder and rape; the government and the administration is apathetic; nothing seems to work.

You know something Mandy, your *Dadiji's* loving me doesn't make her blind to my faults. She never loved me less when she told me to correct myself or helped me to be a better person...

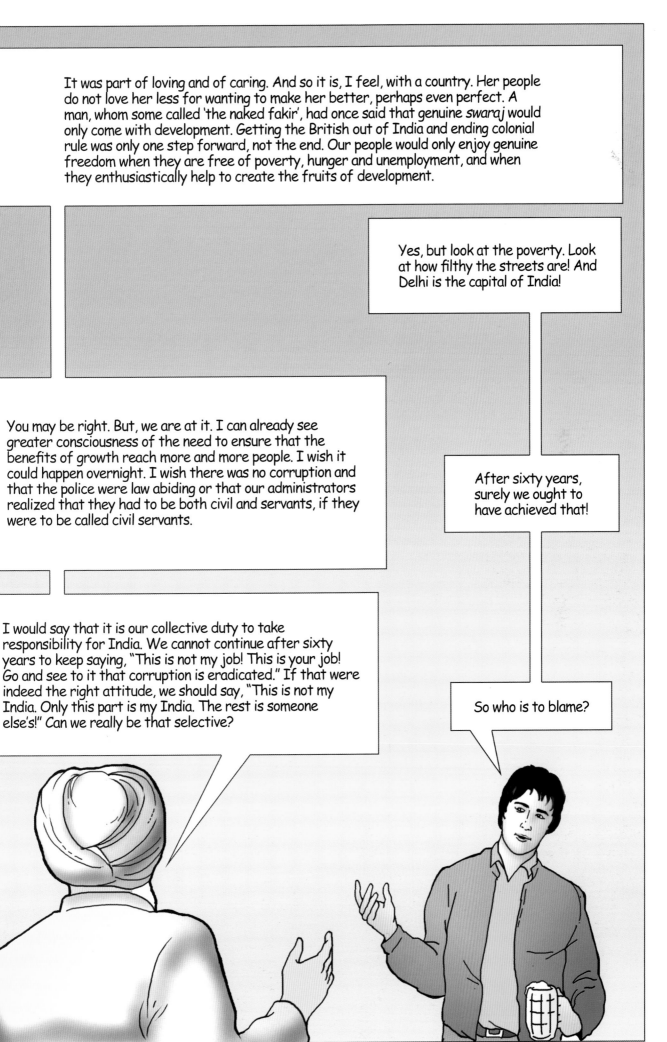

It was part of loving and of caring. And so it is, I feel, with a country. Her people do not love her less for wanting to make her better, perhaps even perfect. A man, whom some called 'the naked fakir', had once said that genuine *swaraj* would only come with development. Getting the British out of India and ending colonial rule was only one step forward, not the end. Our people would only enjoy genuine freedom when they are free of poverty, hunger and unemployment, and when they enthusiastically help to create the fruits of development.

Yes, but look at the poverty. Look at how filthy the streets are! And Delhi is the capital of India!

You may be right. But, we are at it. I can already see greater consciousness of the need to ensure that the benefits of growth reach more and more people. I wish it could happen overnight. I wish there was no corruption and that the police were law abiding or that our administrators realized that they had to be both civil and servants, if they were to be called civil servants.

After sixty years, surely we ought to have achieved that!

I would say that it is our collective duty to take responsibility for India. We cannot continue after sixty years to keep saying, "This is not my job! This is your job! Go and see to it that corruption is eradicated." If that were indeed the right attitude, we should say, "This is not my India. Only this part is my India. The rest is someone else's!" Can we really be that selective?

So who is to blame?

45

Arrey bhai why are you both getting so serious. Listen Mandy, I think you should take a trip and see as much as you can. You don't have to like India but get to know India before you dismiss her. There is much that I do not like about India. And yet, when your parents asked us to go to the US and stay there permanently, I refused. Why? Because this is my home. I would never feel at home anywhere else. Your *Dadaji* and I have never lived in any one place in India for more than three to four years. For us, all the transfers were like moving from one room to another. Today we are in the sitting room, tomorrow in the study, the day after in the veranda. India is like that. She was the roof over our heads. The different cities we visited were like different rooms in a home. And what wonderful friends we made from all parts of India! I find India such a warm and tolerant place. It is truly remarkable, the plural secular ethos of this country.

The US is also a very tolerant society. Look at the various nationalities that live there and the melting pot that has made them Americans.

And yet, after the horrific 9/11 attacks in the US, the first man to be killed in revenge was a Sikh. I think the tolerance and openness of American society is now a thing of the past. Americans have boxed themselves in. They fear the unknown and the unfamiliar. They are not open to a vocabulary or a culture they cannot relate to. They will become increasingly intolerant of other societies and cultures. I am happy to visit but to live there? No thanks.

Even visiting is a problem, Mandy. Visas are not easy to come by. The questioning has become personalized and humiliating. And you always get singled out in a crowd because you look different, you dress different. It's the same even if you were trying to visit an European city. Every visa applicant is seen as a potential immigrant or a terrorist, if they are not from Europe or the US.

I've never faced any discrimination in the US. Lived for as long as I can remember in Chicago and no one has ever treated me differently.

Is that why you call yourself Mandy? What would it be like if you were to say that you are actually Mandeep?

I call myself Mandy because I live and feel like Mandy. Who on earth is Mandeep? I've never met him. I don't feel like him. I don't think like a Mandeep. Why would I want to be called Mandeep if I am not Mandeep?

Quite right! Simrita is just pulling your leg. Come let me tell you about my favourite assignment at the Eastern Command. We lived in Fort William in Calcutta, as it was called then. Amarjit, can you please bring out the album.

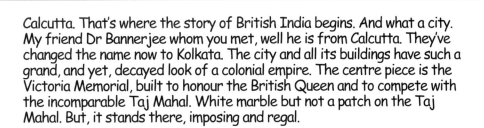

Calcutta. That's where the story of British India begins. And what a city. My friend Dr Bannerjee whom you met, well he is from Calcutta. They've changed the name now to Kolkata. The city and all its buildings have such a grand, and yet, decayed look of a colonial empire. The centre piece is the Victoria Memorial, built to honour the British Queen and to compete with the incomparable Taj Mahal. White marble but not a patch on the Taj Mahal. But, it stands there, imposing and regal.

Your *Dadiji* and I loved going for a walk to the Memorial and eating *jhal muri*. Sunsets over the Howrah Bridge. A stroll on Park Street. Dancing at Moulin Rouge. Dinner at Skyroom or Waldorf's. China Town. New Market. Theatre. Did you know that on any given day there were at least a thousand plays or music concerts in Calcutta? Amarjit saw his first Egyptian mummy in the Calcutta museum.

jhal muri - spicy puffed rice

I loved going to the St Paul's Cathedral. Its solemnity and beauty are simply marvellous. Years ago, I heard Mahalia Jackson sing there. And we once saw a performance of *Murder in the Cathedral* at St Paul's. The Christians have a tremendous influence in Kolkata, in particular. And you can see for yourself the kind of work that Mother Teresa and the sisters have done there. Amarjit was a student at Xavier's Kolkata and I think the education he received there, has made him a better human being.

I had only just got interested in wildlife and Daddy*ji* took us to Sunderbans. This is a photograph of a Royal Bengal Tiger that I took with my camera. I was fourteen years old then...

This is of the crocodile farm. And then, later on, we went to Kaziranga in Assam. And on elephant back, we saw the fabled One-horned Indian Rhino. I could go on and on...

Okay sir. Point taken, I'll give it a shot. Perhaps, Simrita and I could decide where we could go together till Gurinder and Jyoti return from their honeymoon.

If you like, I could take you to my university tomorrow. We could also decide where to visit outside Delhi and get the tickets.

Gmail
by Google BETA

Search Mail   Search the Web   Show search options
Create a filter

Compose Mail

Send   Save Now   Discard

Inbox (2)
Starred ☆
Chats ♡
Sent Mail
Drafts
All Mail
Spam
Trash

Contacts

▼ Quick Contacts
Search, add, or invite
● Mandy
Set status here

● John
Long time...
● Edward
● Gurinder
● Jacks
● Pamela
● William
Yo...
● Bob
Time out...
● Jennifer
● Robert
● Amrita
Add contact   Show all

▼ Labels
Edit labels

To: amy1982@gmail.com

Add Cc | Add Bcc

Subject: Hi...

Attach a file

B I U 𝐹-𝑇T T₂Tᵧ ∞ ⊟ ⊟ ⊡ ⊞ 66 ≡ ≡ ≡ 𝐼 « Plain text   Check spelling ▼

Dear Amy,

Just had the most exhausting day of sightseeing today! U would have
been proud of your big brother. Camera and all that kind of thing! Saw
everything that Delhi has on offer. Tombs, tombs and more tombs.
Even the fort had tombs! I mean what's this obsession with death, I say.
Anyway, good pics especially with the sunset. The colonial architecture
had a sense of imposing grandeur about it. But I must confess, I
preferred the Islamic architecture even though it was all about the dead.

Simrita was my guide and I quite liked having her around. She's good
company. You'd have liked her. She's quite tall and pretty. But na,
not my type. She's very Indian. I am going to her univ tomorrow. The
Jawaharlal Nehru University or JNU. Heard that it is quite modern and
American in its style of teaching and curriculum.

How are Mom and Dad? And how are you? Do drop us mortals a line
if you can take time off your busy schedule? Can't you for once not
manicure your nails?

Love ya
Mandy

▼ Invite a friend
Give Gmail to:

Send Invite 50 left
preview invite

Send   Save Now   Discard

Done   ● Internet

Come and meet my American Indian cousin! He's not as much a weirdo as I thought he would be!

Hi Mandy. We were expecting you and well...didn't quite know what to expect.

Simmi, you've been saying I am a weirdo?

Actually you are. But not as bad as we thought you might be.

Hi Tseten. Simmi told me that you're from India? But you look so different.

He's weird Tseten. It's strange that he has never seen anyone from the north-east of India before?

Hey, look, a peacock dancing!

For me. India is like the colours in a peacock's feather. Each colour is distinct and yet you cannot separate one colour from the other. They weave and mingle one into each other. That is what makes India unique.

So many customs, rituals, languages, diversity. And yet, at the end of the day, they cannot be separated or kept apart. Their individuality comes from collective expression.

What are all these political posters around? Some about Darfur, others on Iraq, Afghanistan and Lebanon. Some about political situation in India.

We are a very political university. I think it is such a good thing. Ever since I came here, I learnt to look at everything in a political manner. My awareness of events around me increased.

During Gurinder's time, he was a member of a group called Free Thinkers. They were apolitical and were not aligned to any political party or grouping.

They took independent views on issues, which were not determined by external political parties. The FT's, as they were called, have more or less disappeared. We are trying to revive them. At our age, we need to think independently. We need to make up our own minds rather than have them shaped by someone sitting outside.

But JNU is basically socialist in its thinking. Issues like humanism and justice concern most students. What about college life for you? What kind of issues do you concern yourself with?

Well, not politics. That's for sure. We do have a student's union but they focus on other student related activities.

Issues such as when the next game is going to be, when should we have our next dance get together, do we rally around and do a programme for the old age home. That sort of thing. Politics? That's not a student thing, I'd say.

And so you would rather not know what happens in Iraq or Sudan or Sarajevo or elsewhere? Is that it? What is *education* if you are not educated about events around the world?

Relax girl. I am sorry about all the sad things happening around but that is not my doing. I go to college to study, meet girls, make friends, drink coffee and play a game of baseball. A date on the weekend. Beer with friends. I didn't join college to change the world.

You're right Sims, the guy is a weirdo. I see Cynthia coming across. Maybe you should introduce him to her. He'll figure out there are North Americans who think different.

Hi guys! Is this your American born *desi* Indian?

Hi there. Haha! Yes he is. Mandy meet Cynthia.

So I take it, you love your mother country!

I hate it!

Ah yes, of course, the poverty, the contradictions, the corruption, the dilemma... much nicer in New York.

Chicago.

Never seen any Afro-Americans lying around with begging bowls in America? The core of jazz and blues music.

Look, it's not the same thing.

What's so different? Why is a hungry black woman different from a hungry brown woman? They die the same, don't they?

Come on Cynthia. Don't give him a bad time on his first outing.

Mandy wants to see India. So we are planning for Goa next week. Why don't Tseten and you join us? I'll ask Gurinder and Jyoti too.

Well...I have a German friend visiting. Dorothee Krueger. She's a student at the South Asia Institute at Heidelberg. I am sure, she and her boyfriend would also like to join us. He's a good guy, even though he is British!

Before Goa, it's Udaipur's turn though...

Tickets are confirmed for a flight to Udaipur and back on the same day. But *Dadiji* insists we stay the night as it is pointless if we don't see Ranakpur or eat lunch there. I have actually asked *her* to join us.

Hey! That's great news.

They catch the next morning's flight...

Udaipur, the City of Lakes, is well known for its Rajput-era palaces; many are resorts now...

They stay at the picturesque Udaipur Lake Hotel surrounded by water on all sides...

Next morning...

Ranakpur is also known by some as the precursor to the Dilwara Temple. It is a beautiful Jain temple with multiple pillars.

The elegance of these multiple pillars is that one of the several pillars is intentionally not parallel to the others. It is a thought-through distortion. *Nazar lag gayi toh*...so the legend goes. Why is that a solitary pillar is inclined, when all the other pillars are perfectly parallel to each other? Sometimes custom and traditional beliefs override architecture. Yet, it continues to be architecturally marvellous even in its imperfection.

Shall we join them for their community lunch?

This is like the *langar* in the gurudwara. Have you tried it in the US?

Yes, everyday for lunch. It's also called hostel food.

Haha! But unlike your hostel food this comes free.

Nazar lag gayi toh - what if an evil eye falls on you; *langar* - the kitchen which serves free food to all people irrespective of their caste, creed, colour or status

They return to Delhi, only to plan for their next day's Agra visit...

I wish *Dadiji* could have come with us to Agra, but it would have gotten too tiring for her. Jogs will be joining us on this trip. Just hope that lazy pig makes it in time for the train.

Next morning...

Hi guys, are we all set to go? Good, then lets board the train. Here we come Taj!

In a few hours we will reach Agra.

Great. Can't wait to see the Taj.

Of course, it is one of the wonders of the world!...so, Boss. You still think that India is bad? Your face yaar, it is so offended by India and everything Indian.

I never said that...tell me Jogs, if I said you could go to the US and stay forever, wouldn't you do so?

Yaar, with my IIT background and IIM, they will take me in the US anytime. But, I have an ego, *yaar*. Will you guarantee that I will not be a second class citizen and that as an Indian, with brown skin, I will receive the same treatment as a white American. Yes? If you guarantee that I will go. But, you need to be the President of America to guarantee this. Visit, yes. Stay, no.

Look at me! I do not face any discrimination.

At your level, you probably don't have a problem. But, I want to be the CEO of a company, partner. I have the qualifications. Will the American system allow such a thing? I don't think so...

I think the US system is quite fair in such matters.

Sure. But I don't think they can quite stomach a non-American making it to the top of the ladder and leaving all these white boys behind. From what I get to hear from my software colleagues, there is a subtle racism that continues to be practiced. America is indeed a melting pot but they select who gets to be melted!...

So, we deal with it another way: as a software company doing well, I look around for American and European companies that I can buy out. Then I can deal with them on my terms.

Ya right! And now you will tell me soon Hindi will become the national language of America!

The train completes its journey to the city of Taj Mahal...

Wow! This is such a mesmerizing sight. I have got to take some snaps.

This breathtaking symbol of eternal love seems to have a life of its own that leaps out of the marble.

Back in Delhi, Mandy checks his e-mail. There's a mail from Amrita. He begins to read...

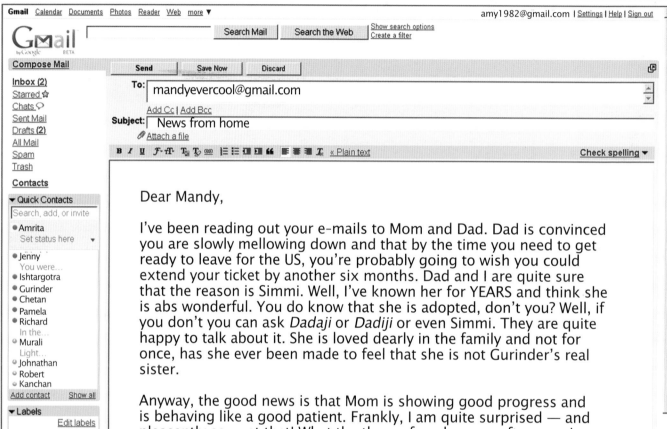

Send   Save Now   Discard

To: mandyevercool@gmail.com

Add Cc | Add Bcc

Subject: News from home

Attach a file

B *I* U 𝓕▾𝕋▾ T▾T▾ ∞ ≣ ≣ ▦ ▦ 66 ≣ ≣ ≣ *I*   « Plain text   Check spelling ▼

Dear Mandy,

I've been reading out your e-mails to Mom and Dad. Dad is convinced you are slowly mellowing down and that by the time you need to get ready to leave for the US, you're probably going to wish you could extend your ticket by another six months. Dad and I are quite sure that the reason is Simmi. Well, I've known her for YEARS and think she is abs wonderful. You do know that she is adopted, don't you? Well, if you don't you can ask *Dadaji* or *Dadiji* or even Simmi. They are quite happy to talk about it. She is loved dearly in the family and not for once, has she ever been made to feel that she is not Gurinder's real sister.

Anyway, the good news is that Mom is showing good progress and is behaving like a good patient. Frankly, I am quite surprised — and pleasantly so — at that! What the three of us do every afternoon is watch old Hindi films! Yes, yes, I know, the sob sob stuff. But, we watched two oldies over the last two days, *Guide* and before that, *Pyasa*. What absolutely wonderful films. Do look around if you can pick up the DVD in Delhi. I think I would like to watch them again and in any case, since you've probably never even heard of them, leave alone seen them, I guess you could jot it down as part of your mandatory learning process on 'what it means to be an Indian'. I promise, you will cry after you've seen the films. Mom and I cried buckets. Dad cleared his throat occasionally and said completely irrelevant things like, 'wonder what Mandy is doing' but I caught him trying to hide his tears at least twice, if not thrice. Hmmmm.

How are *Dadaji* and *Dadiji* and Uncle and Aunty? Do give them our love and tell them that Mom is doing much, much better.

Big hug and don't forget to watch the Beating Retreat.

Amrita

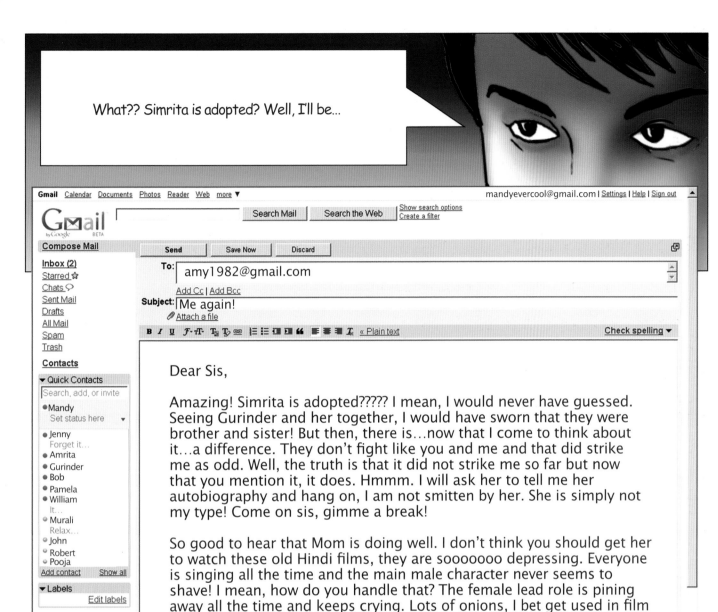

What?? Simrita is adopted? Well, I'll be...

Dear Sis,

Amazing! Simrita is adopted????? I mean, I would never have guessed. Seeing Gurinder and her together, I would have sworn that they were brother and sister! But then, there is…now that I come to think about it…a difference. They don't fight like you and me and that did strike me as odd. Well, the truth is that it did not strike me so far but now that you mention it, it does. Hmmm. I will ask her to tell me her autobiography and hang on, I am not smitten by her. She is simply not my type! Come on sis, gimme a break!

So good to hear that Mom is doing well. I don't think you should get her to watch these old Hindi films, they are sooooooo depressing. Everyone is singing all the time and the main male character never seems to shave! I mean, how do you handle that? The female lead role is pining away all the time and keeps crying. Lots of onions, I bet get used in film making!

Okay, relax. If you want the movies, I'll look for them. Just don't keep adding to the list.

Did I tell you that Simmi took me to see her univ? Quite a nice campus and a bit like the kind of places you have in the US. Met a person from the North East. Wow! Never knew Indians can look *that* different! I thought she was from East Asia. Honest. And there was this total stunner called Cynthia. Yummy! But she's gone and made herself as Indian as an Indian can be. Her accent and good looks give her away! Yes, yes I know, many Indians have become Miss this or Miss that but Cynthia is a dream come true. We might do a visit to Goa together. Will let you know how things go. DON'T you dare read this part out to Mom and Dad. I'll kill you, if you do.

Ended up at the Taj today. Great stuff. But then again, also a tomb. It would be great to see something, for once, that is not a tomb! I am attaching photographs that I took over the last few days.

I still hate India. But, some Indians are not too bad. And some things here are worth a visit.

Big squishy hug. Kisses to Mom and Dad
Mandy

61

Gurinder and Jyoti return from Singapore. Mandy comes down to meet them...

Here comes our Mandeep. Come *puttar*, now you can meet Jyoti more informally.

So happy you could come. Hope your mother has recovered from the fall now.

Amy says that Mom has been a good patient. She is doing well. Thank you.

I spoke to your Mom today. They watched *Pyasa* and *Guide* for the hundredth time! Those two are among my favourites. You may enjoy them. The English subtitles are quite good in *Pyasa*. Very poetic...

I really like Amrita very much. She's such a lovely person. What else did Amrita say? More than that, what all have you been telling her?

Oh just been talking a lot about you all and my trip with Simmi. I was actually surprised, or should I say shocked when Amy told me that Simrita was adopted. She said **she** was surprised that I didn't know that.

Dumbhead, couldn't you figure it out? I mean, just look at my nose. See? So different from Grrrrs. Mine's not pointed. His is. He has what I would say is a proud nose. Mine is typically Bengali. Soft, quiet and not quite there.

Don't be deceived by her nose. She has quite a nose for things!

!?!

Simmi is a Bengali. I was posted in Eastern Command. Her father was a young soldier under me — Dr Bannerjee's son. He died quite young. His wife had died earlier. Simrita became an orphan. Your *Dadiji* and I decided to adopt Simmi. My son and daughter-in-law did me proud. They treated her like their own daughter. We would never have had it otherwise.

Why did Dr Bannerjee give her away?

He is an old, old friend. Simmi is as much Bannerjee *dada's* granddaughter as she is ours. And he didn't give Simmi away. He just gave her a home in addition to his own. He knows how fond I was of his son and he of me.

And you don't find it a problem, Simmi?

Not at all. I spend a lot of time with my real grandparents as well. For me, it is a bonus to have four grandparents who dote on me!

Sarvajit, Dr Bannerjee's only child, died like a soldier on the battlefield in 1971. I was the Commanding Officer. I blamed myself for Sarvajit's death. Perhaps it was my foolhardiness that caused his death. I do not know. Sarvajit was brave and I lost a son. After his death, your *Dadiji* was heart broken. We thought about it for a few days and then, we spoke to Dr Bannerjee and his wife. *Dada* and *Boudi* loved us always. They agreed that Simrita could live with us. Perhaps, he also felt that by looking after Simrita, I can atone for Sarvajit's death. I spoke to my son and my daughter-in-law and Simmi came home to live with us.

dada - elder brother; *Boudi* - brother's wife

And Sim's Mum? I keep seeing Simmi putting garlands on the young couple whose photographs you have there on the wall. Are they Simmi's parents?

Unfortunately, Sarvajit's wife had died much earlier, during child birth.

Yes, they are my parents in the photographs.

Of course, times are changing. You read about old parents being abandoned or left in old age homes to die. Perhaps we should be cautious about getting westernized.

It is horrible! We keep reading reports about how old people and the sick are abandoned because they are seen as a liability. Our values are undergoing a change. Westernization and globalization are okay but not at the cost of the core values that made our society different and worthy of emulation.

Are you talking about the movement from the Hindu undivided family to nuclear units, *Dadiji?*

The Hindu Undivided Family or HUF was a system whereby family members, even after they married, lived together along with their children and their grandchildren. What they earned belonged to the family. Their liabilities were liabilities of the family. In times of stress, the family looked after them. When they did well, the entire family enjoyed the fruits of their success.

Oh! Then what happened?

As time passed, pressures of unemployment took its toll and families had to migrate for work. The 'undivided' family got 'divided' and nuclear units were set up. Still the links between brothers and sisters and cousins and uncles and aunts remained very, very strong. Over time, these links have weakened. The old family values have started making less sense as nuclear families have started thinking about themselves and their own security rather than that of the greater family.

Mr Bannerjee and his wife arrive at lunch time...

Bhalo theko. Brought you *hilsa* fish. Straight from Kolkata.

At lunch, everyone tucks into the *hilsa* with their fingers. Mandy is unable to deal with the fish. He musters courage...

Auw! This fish has many bones.

Many...but what a fish!

Bhalo theko - stay well, standard form of blessing by an elder; *hilsa* - type of bony river fish (a speciality)

Yawn! Now that we are through with lunch, what's the programme today?

Match. We play a game to warm up and then, relax and watch the test.

Match? What match?

What a weirdo!

Oye pappe! Cricket silly. We are playing England and we would have lost the first test if it weren't for the rains.

For the first time, everyone in India was happy with global warming and the unprecedented rains!

That's a silly game, isn't it? Lasts for days and days and you could end up with a draw. Sorry, but it's true.

Just get him into the field right away before I bowl him a bouncer Simmi.

Mandy steps on to the cricket pitch and plays the first ball which almost takes his head off...

Hey! This isn't a baseball game buddy. You need to watch the ball and think.

Go ahead... make my day...

Provoked, Mandy strikes again with all his might...

I will show you what I can do. It's just a silly game.

Wah!! How did you do that?

Later that afternoon, all gather to watch the second test match telecast...

Boy! This is just like baseball excitement at home.

198 all out and India wins Hurrah! Hurrah!

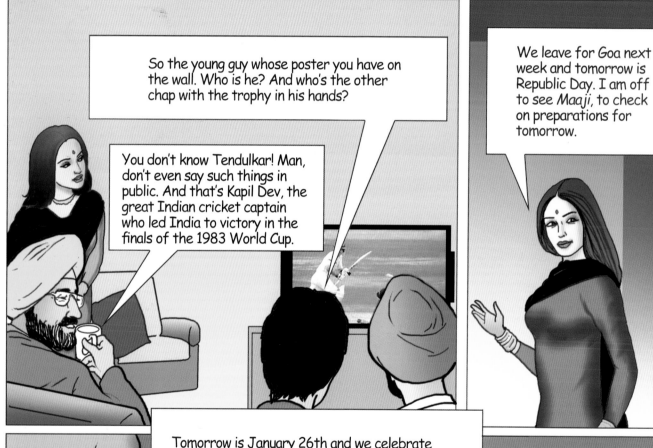

So the young guy whose poster you have on the wall. Who is he? And who's the other chap with the trophy in his hands?

We leave for Goa next week and tomorrow is Republic Day. I am off to see *Maaji*, to check on preparations for tomorrow.

You don't know Tendulkar! Man, don't even say such things in public. And that's Kapil Dev, the great Indian cricket captain who led India to victory in the finals of the 1983 World Cup.

Tomorrow is January 26th and we celebrate Republic Day. It is a national celebration. If you kids would like to watch the celebrations, I have passes that you can use. I would prefer to be at home with your *Dadiji* and watch it on TV. All this security checking and reaching two hours before, is difficult at my age.

Watching it on TV is more fun, I think. Simmi, Kulvinder and I will make pakoras and samosas, we have already marinated the meat for tikkas and kebabs. Gurinder will, no doubt, take care of the beer.

Dadu and *Thakum* will be coming over, as always, and will bring *Bangla khana*. I've told *Thakum*, I am missing fried *karelas*, *rohu* fish in yogurt, tomato chutney and *mishti doi*.

They always bring food for an army! My parents are also going to be here and it should be fun.

On 26th January morning, everyone settles to watch the Republic Day parade...

Dadu - Grandfather; *Thakum* - Grandmother; *karela* - bitter gourd; *mishti doi* - sweetened yogurt

I hope you enjoyed the parade Mandy. I have always found the Beating Retreat to be magnificent. Would you like to see it on the 29th? Gurinder could try and get some tickets.

Sure, I would love to watch it.

I've arranged for banana leaves instead of plates. A delightful traditional Bengali lunch is ready for all. Come let's eat.

Mandy struggles with a knife and a fork. Simrita teaches him how to eat with hands...

Start with the fried aubergines. I would recommend the *luchis*, which is like a *puri* but made out of white flour. On the side, keep the tomato chutney for dipping into with your fingers. You CAN'T do this with a knife and fork, silly! That's a banana leaf and you will cut it with the knife!!

Mandy gingerly tries it out with his fingers...

Hmmm, it doesn't taste bad, actually it's good. Very good. Very very good. Actually, simply superb!

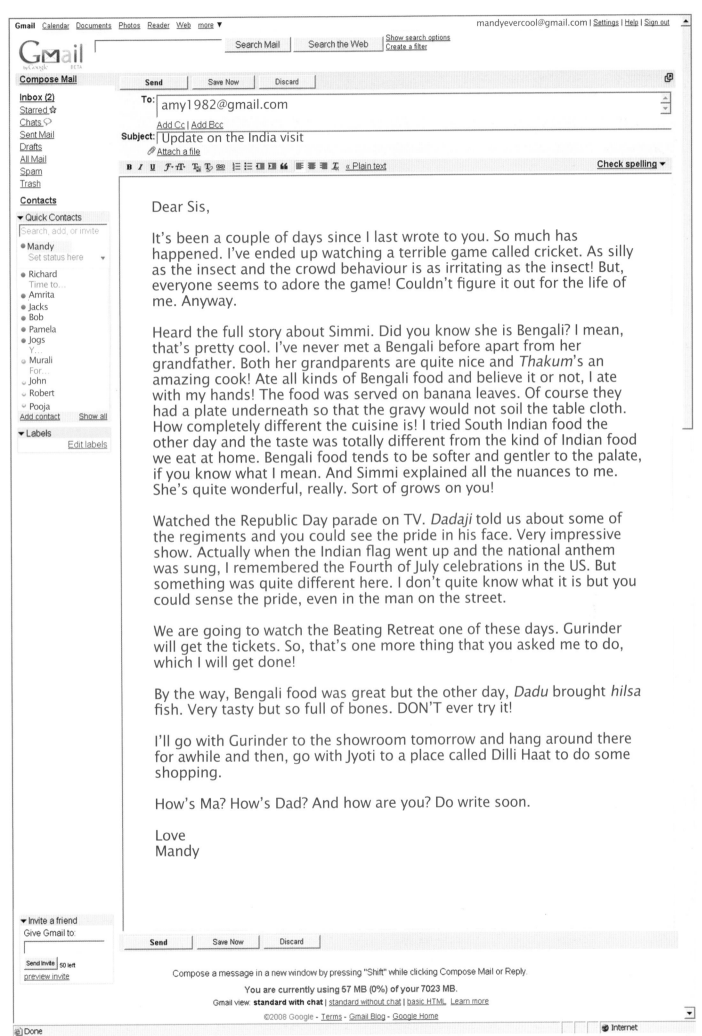

Gmail Calendar Documents Photos Reader Web more ▼   mandyevercool@gmail.com | Settings | Help | Sign out

Gmail
by Google BETA

Search Mail   Search the Web   Show search options
                                 Create a filter

Compose Mail   Send   Save Now   Discard

Inbox (2)   To: amy1982@gmail.com
Starred ☆
Chats ♡   Add Cc | Add Bcc
Sent Mail   Subject: Update on the India visit
Drafts   ∅ Attach a file
All Mail
Spam   B I U F·T· T₁T₂∞ |≡ ≔ ⊡ ⊡ 66 ▆ ▆ ▆ I « Plain text   Check spelling ▼
Trash

Contacts

▼ Quick Contacts   Dear Sis,

Search, add, or invite   It's been a couple of days since I last wrote to you. So much has
● Mandy   happened. I've ended up watching a terrible game called cricket. As silly
  Set status here   ▼   as the insect and the crowd behaviour is as irritating as the insect! But,
● Richard   everyone seems to adore the game! Couldn't figure it out for the life of
  Time to…   me. Anyway.
● Amrita
● Jacks   Heard the full story about Simmi. Did you know she is Bengali? I mean,
● Bob   that's pretty cool. I've never met a Bengali before apart from her
● Pamela   grandfather. Both her grandparents are quite nice and *Thakum*'s an
● Jogs   amazing cook! Ate all kinds of Bengali food and believe it or not, I ate
  Y…   with my hands! The food was served on banana leaves. Of course they
● Murali   had a plate underneath so that the gravy would not soil the table cloth.
  For…   How completely different the cuisine is! I tried South Indian food the
● John   other day and the taste was totally different from the kind of Indian food
● Robert   we eat at home. Bengali food tends to be softer and gentler to the palate,
● Pooja   if you know what I mean. And Simmi explained all the nuances to me.
Add contact Show all   She's quite wonderful, really. Sort of grows on you!

▼ Labels   Watched the Republic Day parade on TV. *Dadaji* told us about some of
         Edit labels   the regiments and you could see the pride in his face. Very impressive
                          show. Actually when the Indian flag went up and the national anthem
                          was sung, I remembered the Fourth of July celebrations in the US. But
                          something was quite different here. I don't quite know what it is but you
                          could sense the pride, even in the man on the street.

                          We are going to watch the Beating Retreat one of these days. Gurinder
                          will get the tickets. So, that's one more thing that you asked me to do,
                          which I will get done!

                          By the way, Bengali food was great but the other day, *Dadu* brought *hilsa*
                          fish. Very tasty but so full of bones. DON'T ever try it!

                          I'll go with Gurinder to the showroom tomorrow and hang around there
                          for awhile and then, go with Jyoti to a place called Dilli Haat to do some
                          shopping.

                          How's Ma? How's Dad? And how are you? Do write soon.

                          Love
                          Mandy

▼ Invite a friend
Give Gmail to:

                    Send   Save Now   Discard

Send Invite | 50 left
preview invite   Compose a message in a new window by pressing "Shift" while clicking Compose Mail or Reply.

                          You are currently using 57 MB (0%) of your 7023 MB.
                    Gmail view: **standard with chat** | standard without chat | basic HTML Learn more
                          ©2008 Google - Terms - Gmail Blog - Google Home

🔊 Done   🌐 Internet

Mobile Phones, IPods, Mp3 players of so many brands!!! I say, Gurinder, never thought you could get all this stuff in India! Really cool!

You get almost everything here these days. Many international companies are here and we manufacture much of the stuff here in India. Things will only get better.

There was a time when people would pick up electronic items from Dubai or Hongkong or Singapore. Not anymore. It's cheaper here.

Just then Jyoti arrives...

Come on Mandy, let's go. Sorry I am late. Simmi will join us in Dilli Haat and Tseten and Cynthia might also tag along.

Lucky devil! You have four girls to take care of! Enjoy yourselves.

I hope your stay is comfortable and that your memories of India are not going to be totally negative.

So, this sis of mine, has spoken to you.

Joe? Can I call you Joe?

Yes, of course. Amrita and I are old friends. She told me before you came that you were totally reluctant to come here.

Sure, if it makes you more comfortable. Though I must confess I prefer my original name.

Jyoti, means light...that's a lovely *dupatta*. I will buy it.

Light? Wow! That's pretty cool. Do all Indian names have meanings?

Very often. Some people opt for names based on Gods, like Lakshmi or Ganesh or Kartik or Arjun.

Hmm... interesting curios! This place is so colorful and I love the sense of happy chaos all around.

dupatta - traditional Indian scarf worn by women

Gurinder told me that you wondered how he and I could get married without being in love.

I'll kill Gurinder. That was a private thing between him and me.

Oh, don't worry about it! But falling in love is not denied to you when you have an arranged marriage.

That's true, but once you get married, you are stuck!

So you feel we should begin by trying to live together for awhile? Sleep together? Run a home together? Become partners, till we finally agree, after several years, to go in for a commitment? Would that be the way out?

That sounds crass. But yes, at least persons who are getting married to one another should know each other. People live together, without getting married, in many countries. It gives you an opportunity to gauge whether the person is truly your life partner.

And then the three ladies arrive...

Hi you two! Done any shopping?

Hi everyone! We've been having an enjoyable chat about arranged marriages versus love marriages.

Like in Western countries? By that time, life could well near be over and the couple would still be undecided!

Hi girls! With four ladies to hang out with, boy I will surely get bullied!

It's a cultural thing, I guess.

It's fun time Dilli Haat style before the three see off Tseten and Cynthia...

They go to watch the Beating Retreat where Gurinder meets them...

The lucky devil is back! Four pretty girls and all to yourself! I would have happily offered to be the baggage handler or driver!!

Had a fabulous time, partner. Got to know Joe better.

The ceremony begins...

Hear the bell chime the notes of the psalm *Abide With Me*. That was Gandhi*ji*'s favourite hymn.

Back at home...

Tomorrow I will take you to pay homage to a great man who shook the mightiest empire with the power of his mind and the simplicity of his thought. Many call him the *Mahatma* but I can only think of him as *Bapuji* for he was like a father to all Indians.

You are getting special treatment Mandy. *Dadaji* is very particular whom he takes to Rajghat and to the house where *Gandhiji* was assassinated.

I am honoured...

Next day they visit Birla House...

He is also known as the 'Father of the Nation'.

At Rajghat, they pay a silent tribute with flowers, to one of the greatest human beings who walked this earth...

You are leaving tomorrow for Goa. Better get your packing done. For the journey, I thought you might find the time to read *Bapuji's* autobiography. Some day you might read more about the man who became the *Mahatma*.

Thank you so much *Dadaji*. I will surely make the time.

Dadaji, Does anyone bother about Gandhi anymore?... I mean...you read about peace and non-violence and compassion and tolerance... but who cares? Look around and all you see is poverty and violence...does Gandhi matter even in the country of his birth?

You speak the truth. But, that does not mean that there isn't another way. Whether Gandhi matters or whether his thoughts are still relevant are in no way a reflection on his thoughts or his philosophy but on us. If the philosophy behind the *Dhamapadda* and the *Gita* and the *Granth Sahib* and the *Bible* and the *Quran* are not followed, does that make these holy books irrelevant?

This is going to be a long debate, I can see. I better go and pack.

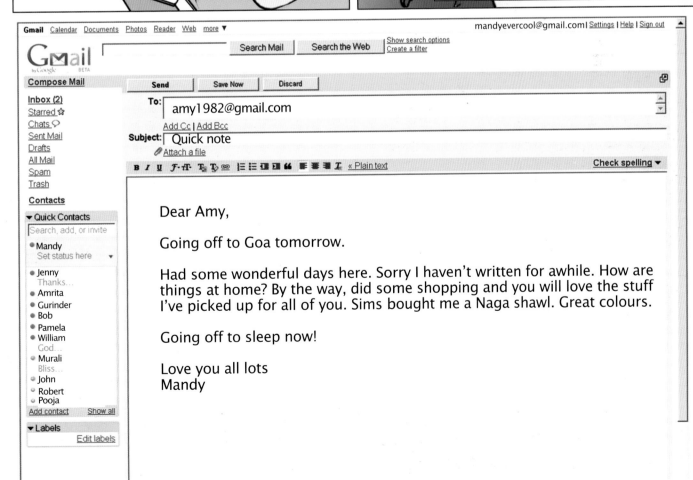

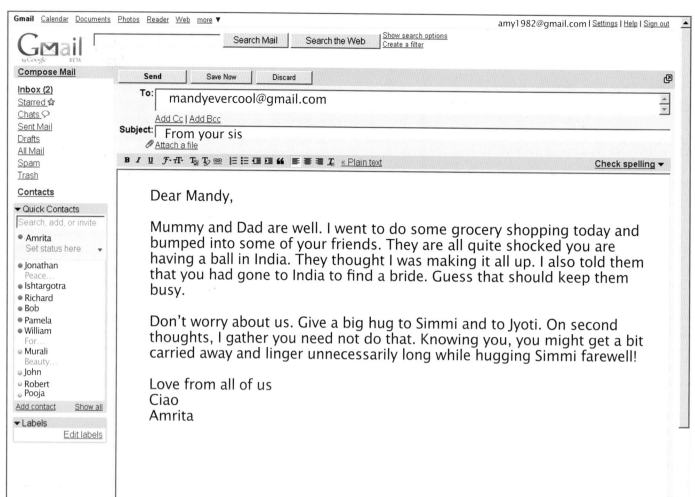

Gmail BETA

Search Mail   Search the Web   Show search options / Create a filter

Compose Mail

Inbox (2)
Starred ☆
Chats ♡
Sent Mail
Drafts
All Mail
Spam
Trash

Contacts

▼ Quick Contacts
Search, add, or invite
● Amrita
  Set status here
● Jonathan
  Peace…
● Ishtargotra
● Richard
● Bob
● Pamela
● William
  For…
○ Murali
  Beauty…
○ John
○ Robert
○ Pooja
Add contact   Show all

▼ Labels
        Edit labels

Send   Save Now   Discard

To: mandyevercool@gmail.com
Add Cc | Add Bcc
Subject: From your sis
Attach a file

B I U F·T T T ∞ ≣ ≣ ▤ ▤ 66 ≣ ≣ ≣ I « Plain text   Check spelling ▼

Dear Mandy,

Mummy and Dad are well. I went to do some grocery shopping today and bumped into some of your friends. They are all quite shocked you are having a ball in India. They thought I was making it all up. I also told them that you had gone to India to find a bride. Guess that should keep them busy.

Don't worry about us. Give a big hug to Simmi and to Jyoti. On second thoughts, I gather you need not do that. Knowing you, you might get a bit carried away and linger unnecessarily long while hugging Simmi farewell!

Love from all of us
Ciao
Amrita

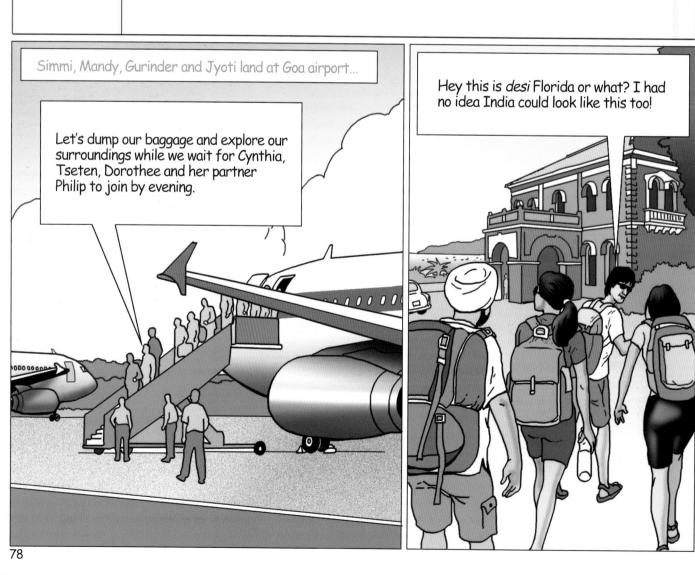

Simmi, Mandy, Gurinder and Jyoti land at Goa airport...

Let's dump our baggage and explore our surroundings while we wait for Cynthia, Tseten, Dorothee and her partner Philip to join by evening.

Hey this is *desi* Florida or what? I had no idea India could look like this too!

It's sun, sand and sea time...

Later that evening...

Hi guys, welcome to Goa.

Hey, good to see you.

Let's go to the nearest Goan Café.

Guys meet Doro. She is into films and is studying about the entertainment sector in India, particularly Bollywood. She's been telling us the most fascinating story about how Bollywood is a rage in Germany and you even have Bollywood films on prime time TV dubbed in German!

You mean Shah Rukh Khan says, *Guten Morgan?*

Yea and much else too. They've managed to get Germans whose voices more or less match those of all the leading actors. The one who does Amitabh Bachchan is quite good and has the same baritone quality!

So what's with this Bollywood thing in Germany? Why do they like it?

I think Germans initially found the song and dance quite hilarious but they love the simple story line and the fabulous colours of India. And the women are sooooo pretty! Bollywood is about the human values that we have all been brought up with and somehow lost on the way. Love. Family. Grief. Bonding.

I find Indian films soppy and silly. Give me a good American film anytime.

But India has the biggest entertainment industry in the world. Almost a thousand films are made every year.

Indian films have gone global and their success and popularity cannot be ignored anymore.

I totally agree with you Philip. Let's order for the food now. I'm starving.

I'll have *vindaloo* with rice.

Why not get a couple of crabs?

Likewise. Perhaps we could order a Goan prawn curry.

It's easiest to order a few plates of pomfret, prawns and crabs and we can all tuck in.

vindaloo - a spicy Portuguese curry in red wine

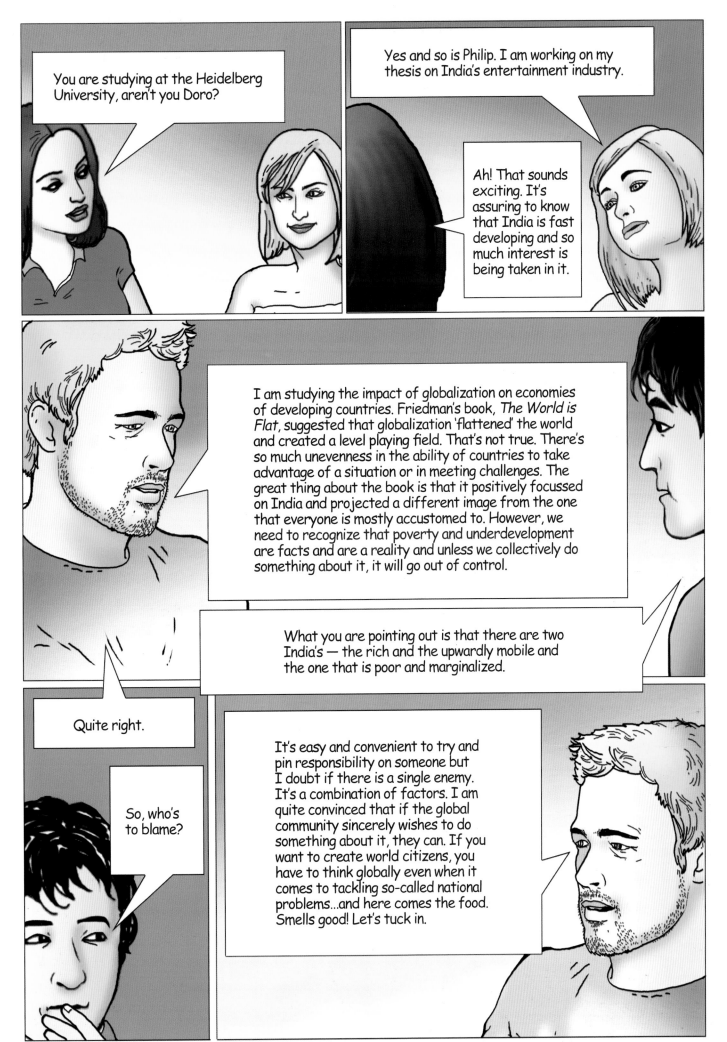

Baba studied in St Xavier's Kolkata. The Jesuits are a big influence, especially in education.

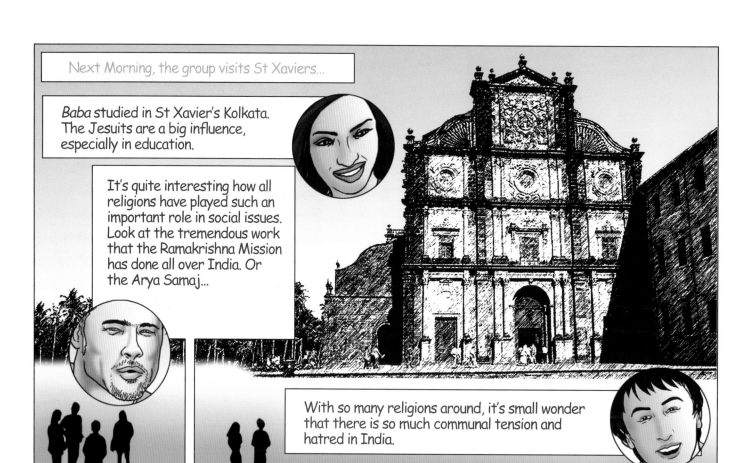

It's quite interesting how all religions have played such an important role in social issues. Look at the tremendous work that the Ramakrishna Mission has done all over India. Or the Arya Samaj...

With so many religions around, it's small wonder that there is so much communal tension and hatred in India.

Actually, there are communal tensions everywhere. Religious fanaticism is not the monopoly of some countries or cultures. I would say that pluralism and secularism is the USP of India. Of course, one would like to see greater tolerance and a separation of religion from politics.

As a Buddhist, I must confess that what I find truly remarkable about India is her religious diversity. I agree with Philip that one would like to see greater tolerance and I do hope it comes with education and development.

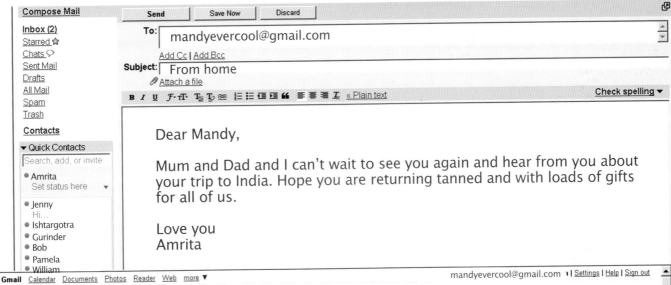

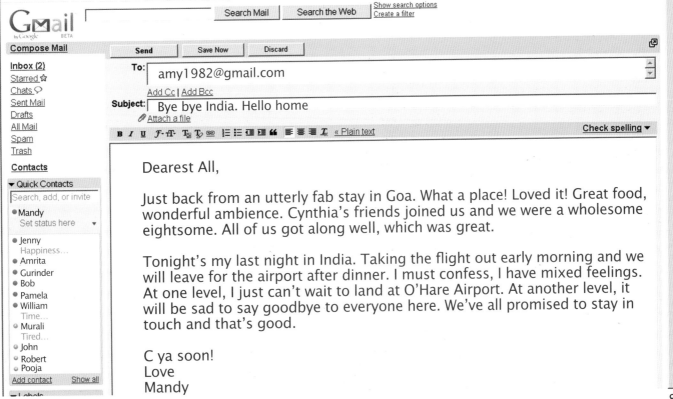

I say partner, you need to get married. It will help make you a little more organized.

And of course, the wedding would need to be in India.

Hmph! I have no intention of getting married anytime soon. And in any case, it has to be a love marriage.

Ah yes, of course. But then, does our young Mandy have time to fall in love?

Really Sims! Actually the blondes are not as pretty as you?

Na, he's too busy chasing blondes in Chicago.

Hey, get the drinks flowing. In a few hours you will be back in Chicago. We will miss you *beta*.

This small packet is for your parents. Typical Bengali sweets. They will love them.

What are those, *Dadi*?

Pickles. Wrap these up carefully, so that the bottles don't break. Now that you are packed, let us sit together for awhile and chat.

I am so glad you could come to India and be with us. Weddings and occasions are important for all of us to be together but even otherwise, it is very important to keep in touch. I think we should try our best to meet at least once every year. It's such a good feeling to wait for the reunion, to count days, to make plans on what we all would do when we meet.

Four weeks ago, I would have dismissed the idea. But now, I do feel it will be a wonderful thing to do. Perhaps you all could come over to Chicago later in the year. Mum and Dad and Amy would be thrilled.

We are growing old. It is the responsibility of youngsters to come and see us.

You both are not growing old. Don't ever say that again!

Dadaji, Dadiji, you don't need to come to the airport. It's cold and quite late. You need to rest.

Your *Dadiji* and I would feel happier seeing off our grandson. Come along.

They head to the airport...

Hey Mandy, look around for the last time and say bye to the city. Something tells me you will come back soon, haha!

It's time for Mandy to go in for security check...

Do keep in touch *puttar* and next time bring your parents and sister along.

Take care buddy. Call me once you reach there...

...or we would worry.

Bhalo theko! Be happy and stay healthy.

You'll keep in touch, won't you?

Yes, I surely will. Thank you for everything.

Indian by Choice

From around the mid-sixties, India witnessed what many, in Indian circles, described as 'the brain drain'; bright young Indian students moved on for higher studies to the US, in particular, but also to the UK (as a second choice), after completing their preliminary studies in engineering, medicine and science from some of India's premiere educational institutions. Indian policy makers were alarmed because they felt that the benefit of the education that these very bright youngsters had received in India would now be denied to her and would be of advantage to the US, the UK or the receiving country. India's brain drain would be a brain gain for another country. As a result, there was a fair amount of informal talk that penalties and disincentives ought to be introduced in the form of bank guarantees to prevent such out-migration. Brain drain was seen as a serious national problem.

These students, who started moving out in the sixties and the seventies, successfully completed higher studies in the US and elsewhere. Many opted to work in the US, obtained the green card, came back to India briefly to marry, and then settled down in the US. They subsequently bought homes with large gardens in the suburbs. They did well, in comparison to the life they would have led in India, but not in comparison to what many thought they were actually capable of in their adopted country! A handful hung on to their Indian passports and thus, their nationality. They were, naturally, easily distinguishable from the other and very large group of Indians, who also migrated to the US, ostensibly to seek political asylum but essentially for economic reasons. Both groups did well economically and in relative terms, were seen as 'success stories' back home. India in the sixties and in the seventies had precious little to offer in terms of job opportunities or upward economic mobility.

These migrants came home to India, initially every year, to meet their aging parents and other siblings. Gradually, their visits decreased. Their parents went across to the US on tickets that their children would send them. By the time these migrants were around fifty years of age, it was time for that bearer of bad news: the dreaded late night telephone call. Once the parents passed on, their bonds with India loosened and the incentive to visit India rapidly decreased; in a sense, the umbilical cord was irreversibly cut. Only nostalgia remained. Perhaps, even a little bitterness.

In differing ways, the migrant Indians adapted. Some quickly picked up the American twang so that they could blend in their new and adopted surroundings and did not stand out as sore thumbs. Their accents dramatically changed and became totally indistinguishable from that of native Americans. They learnt the intricacies of baseball and American football, games that they were totally unfamiliar with. They embraced the American way of life along with French fries and hot dog. Many changed their names: Mandeep became Mandy, Sandeep-Sandy, Parminder-Pamela, Jaikishan-Jackson, Harminder-Harry, Janardhan-Johnny. Places like New York, Jackson Heights and neighbouring areas or New Jersey, some two hours away from New York City, became home to the majority of Indians. In cities like London, they created their own ghettos or 'little Indias' where they lived in the world of curries and sarees. The language of everyday conversation was chaste Punjabi or Gujarati, depending on the congregation.

The more educated and professional Indians sent their children to Ivy League schools and colleges — Harvard and Princeton and Columbia in the US or to Oxford and Cambridge and LSE in the UK. Their children moved on to good jobs after graduation and competed on equal terms with other American and European professionals.

Yet for the parents, there was something acutely lacking. Many had left India as young and fresh students and looked at the US as the land of opportunity. They hoped to not only strike it rich but to also achieve great professional heights. Some did. But the majority found themselves stuck in the middle rung. The top job always remained elusive. They slowly moved on to 'self-employment' jobs either as engineers or in software or as consultants. Complete and unqualified acceptance in American society was never quite there; somehow, something seemed to be lacking, somehow there was always a distance from their American counterparts and office colleagues. The ice could never be totally broken. And yet, they could never put their finger on what it was that was missing.

An overwhelming sense of 'Indianness' swept over them. They sought out Indian culture and it is now well documented that several schools of classical Indian dance and music sprouted all over to cater to the children of these migrants. They regularly met with other Indians to speak in their mother tongue and to eat traditional Indian food. They contributed unquestioningly to the construction of temples and gurudwaras in their adopted countries. The celebration of Indian festivals became a major outing and an event where they re-created what they had left behind and now, sorely missed. Increasingly, they became passionately 'Indian' in their attitude and in their behaviour.

The occasional news of racist behaviour towards Indians agitated and mobilized them. It also made them identify less and less with their adopted home; they began to feel like outsiders and realized that they never had been permitted to fully assimilate despite their best attempts. There was always a 'you are not one of us' attitude — subtle but thinly, very thinly, veiled that confronted them in several situations. Then, four days after 9/11, a Sikh gas station owner was gunned down in a revenge attack. Suddenly, the Indian immigrant felt vulnerable, even betrayed. While the Indian immigrants were the second wealthiest immigrants in the US and contributed substantial funds to American political parties, the land they called home had somehow failed to understand and accept them or their culture. This was the ultimate betrayal.

Unknown to them, since the late eighties and early nineties, India was ushering in a quiet revolution through the liberalization of its economy. Growth figures inched up from the sixties and seventies figure of a modest 3.5 per cent to around 5.8 per cent and continued this ascendancy to 7–8 per cent, with credible forecasts that 10 per cent might be attainable in the realistic future. It was predicted that by 2040, India would be the third largest economy after the US and China. The unshackling of the Indian economy seemed to release the pent-up Indian entrepreneurial talent and a huge surge of Indian enterprise captured global imagination. The mushrooming of call centres and the concept of BPOs became synonymous with India. Companies like Infosys and Wipro became household names; Bangalore represented the 'new India'. Indian industry seemed to have finally found its rightful place and turned its eyes towards mergers and acquisitions. Mittal, Tata and a host of Indian companies now moved in to acquire European and American companies; what is particularly fascinating is that they turned the fortunes of these companies around and thereby, debunked the protectionist argument that such acquisitions would result in job losses and bad management practices. For the Indians all over, this was a cause of celebration and joy and, more importantly, of pride.

Reportage on India in the American and European press dramatically changed with positive coverage by highly respected journalists and commentators, particularly Thomas Friedman, who not only wrote a series of articles for *New York Times* on the 'new India' but also a book with a provocative title *The World is Flat*, which essentially was a treatise on the positive effects of globalization; he used India as a dramatic success story. While there are many who disagreed with Friedman's thesis about the world having been flattened as a result of globalization, he undoubtedly put the focus, in a hugely positive manner, on India.

India's steadfast adherence to democracy and the development of its strategic partnership with the US, positively impacted on the global image of the 'new India'. For several years, Western scholars have drawn attention to the fact that while India's democratic institutions have consistently been strengthened, this has simply not been the case with countries in India's neigbourhood and those that were earlier part of the subcontinent. This has often triggered debates on what might be *that* critical element or 'Indianness' that embraced democracy when at least two of India's large neighbours simply failed to succeed on that front. Furthermore, the possible strategic understanding between India and the US has also found positive echoes in Europe, as well, and this should augur positively on all aspects of bilateral relations, between India and Europe, both at the governmental and people-to-people level.

The fall-out of the above has been a surge of 'national' pride among the vast non-resident Indian community. A few years ago, an e-mail spread like wildfire on the internet; it was titled *Proud to be an Indian* and the text is, illustratively, reproduced below from the internet:

PROUD TO BE AN INDIAN
LET THE WORLD KNOW WHAT WE STAND FOR

- There are 3.22 million Indians in America.

- 38% of doctors in America are Indians.

- 12% of scientists in America are Indians.

- 36% of NASA employees are Indians.

- 34% of MICROSOFT employees are Indians.

- 28% of IBM employees are Indians.

- 17% of INTEL employees are Indians.

- 13% of XEROX employees are Indians.

- You may know some of these facts. These facts were recently published in a German Magazine, which deals with WORLD HISTORY FACTS ABOUT INDIA:

- India never invaded any country in her last 10000 years of history.

- India invented the Number System.

- Aryabhatta invented zero.

- The World's first university was established in Takshila in 700BC. More than 10,500 students from all over the world studied more than 60 subjects. The University of Nalanda built in the 4th century BC was one of the greatest achievements of ancient India in the field of education.

- Sanskrit is the mother of all the European languages. Sanskrit is the most suitable language for computer software as reported in Forbes magazine, July 1987.

- Ayurveda is the earliest school of medicine known to humans. Charaka, the father of medicine consolidated Ayurveda 2500 years ago. Today Ayurveda is fast regaining its rightful place in our civilization.

- Although modern images of India often show poverty and lack of development, India was the richest country on earth until the time of British invasion in the early 17th Century.

- The art of navigation was born in the river Sindh 6000 years ago. The very word navigation is derived from the Sanskrit word *Navgatih*. The Word navy is also derived from Sanskrit *Nou*.

- Bhaskaracharya calculated the time taken by the earth to orbit the sun hundreds of years before the astronomer Smart. Time taken by earth to orbit the sun: (5th century) 365.258756484 days.

- Budhayana first calculated the value of pi, and he explained the concept of what is known as the Pythagorean Theorem. He discovered this in the 6th century long before the European mathematicians. Algebra, trigonometry and calculus came from India; quadratic equations were by Sridharacharya in the 11th century ; the largest numbers the Greeks and the Romans used were 10^6(10 to the power of 6) whereas Hindus used numbers as big as 10^{53} (10 to the power of 53) with specific names as Early as 5000 BCE during the Vedic period. Even today, the largest used number is Tera 10^{12}(10 to the power of 12).

- According to the Gemological Institute of America, up until 1896, India was the only source for diamonds to the world. USA based IEEE has proved what has been a century-old suspicion in the world scientific community that the pioneer of wireless communication was Prof Jagdeesh Bose and not Marconi.

- The earliest reservoir and dam for irrigation was built in Saurashtra. According to Saka King Rudradaman I of 150 CE a beautiful lake called 'Sudarshana' was constructed on the hills of Raivataka during Chandragupta Maurya's time.

- Chess (*Shataranja* or *AshtaPada*) was invented in India.

- Sushruta is the father of surgery. 2600 years ago he and health scientists of his time conducted complicated surgeries like cesarean, cataract, artificial limbs, fractures, urinary stones and even plastic surgery and brain surgery. Usage of anesthesia was well known in ancient India. Over 125 surgical equipments were used. Deep knowledge of anatomy, etiology, embryology, digestion,metabolism, genetics and immunity is also found in many texts.

- When many cultures were only nomadic forest dwellers over 5000 years ago, Indians established Harappan culture in Sindhu Valley (Indus Valley Civilization). The place value system, the decimal system was developed in India in 100 BC.

QUOTES ABOUT INDIA

- Albert Einstein said: We owe a lot to the Indians, who taught us how to count, without which no worthwhile scientific discovery could have been made.

- Mark Twain said: India is the cradle of the human race, the birthplace of human speech, the mother of history, the grandmother of legend, and the great grandmother of tradition. Our most valuable and most astructive materials in the history of man are treasured up in India only.

- French scholar Romain Rolland said: If there is one place on the face of earth where all the dreams of living men have found a home from the very earliest days when man began the dream of existence, it is India.

- Hu Shih, former Ambassador of China to USA said: India conquered and dominated China culturally for 20 centuries without ever having to send a single soldier across her border.

- All the above is just the TIP of the iceberg, the list could be endless. BUT, if we don't see even a glimpse of that great India in the India that we see today, it clearly means that we are not working up to our potential and that if we do, we could once again be an ever shining and inspiring country setting a bright path for rest of the world to follow. I Hope you enjoyed it and work towards the welfare of INDIA. PROUD to be an INDIAN.

The text of the e-mail reflects a deep sense of suddenly acquired 'national' pride. It is euphoric and celebratory in language though some of the information might be over-exaggerated. This is perhaps a direct consequence of a feeling of desolation and alienation from the adopted country, and thus a sudden realization of the achievements of the mother country (India) and the recognition that it is globally receiving. Fascinatingly, it is not simply a sense of national pride at India's past and present achievements that the text refers to but also a call to action by *all* Indians, both resident and non-resident, to join hands and collectively let India attain her rightful place in the comity of nations.

A visible shift appears to have taken place. This has resulted in acknowledging 'Indianness'. Mandeep began by chosing to be called Mandy, so that he might be accepted by his American friends, neighbours and acquaintances; today, it is Mandy, who willingly opts to be called Mandeep: he became Indian by *choice*.

II

The book is essentially in the style of a graphic novel, though it experiments by deploying three different styles of expression — the graphic illustrations, text (through e-mails that Mandy receives and sends, and this chapter) and photographs. The target audience is varied; at one level, it reaches out to the non-resident younger generation of Indians and to the young professionals who are increasingly having to engage with India for business and other reasons, at another level, it tells the story of India to the resident Indians, to our young generation and to the tourist. Obliquely, it tries to answer the question: what is India? While there is pride in India, as evinced through the internet message posted above, there is also a great deal of confusion and lack of knowledge about India, a number of unanswered questions, and indeed, fears. The book candidly acknowledges this and the fact that India's success story has many more miles to go, that poverty and hunger continue to plague us, that corruption and red tape are still deeply entrenched and stymie good governance and that India's secular ethos is tested time and time again. Through storytelling, the novel attempts to respond to these questions and to the dilemma many youngsters are facing of returning to India and discovering their roots: Is the India of their imagination akin to the India of day-to-day living? Would they be able to adjust to life in India after so many years?

To be fair, India is not easy, neither for the middle class nor for the poorer Indians nor indeed for the returning non-resident. For one, I have never quite figured out how an Indian can dramatically change once he leaves foreign shores! He becomes loud, excessively garrulous, completely impervious to rules and regulations, and basically a nuisance. It has always been a matter of great frustration for me to hear the jingle jangle of mobile phones on Indian aircrafts as the air hostess advises passengers not to switch on their mobile phones till the aircraft comes to a perfect halt. Would they flout these regulations as they fly into Chicago or Washington or London? Of course not. Why do they do it in India? I have no idea whatsoever. This, naturally, extends beyond the use of mobile phones to basic behavioural patterns. Once I had the temerity to ask an Indian, who was a US national, why he was behaving the way he was and his answer was quite an eye-opener for me, "*Aare ji, yeh to India hain ji, sub kuch chalta hain!*" loosely translated, "This is India, everything goes!"

It has often been said, and rightly so, that India is a hierarchical society and one that, as a result, survives on networking and in building the 'right' connections and contacts. It comes as no surprise that the obvious and immediate question of new acquaintances has usually been, "Who is your father? What does he do? Where do you live?" These three questions 'place' people in context rather rapidly and thereafter, networking begins! It's quite incredible really how the system works and how whom you know can come in handy and actually open doors and get things done, including getting the otherwise lethargic bureaucratic system to work, indeed, at all levels; a phone call and the machinery swings into action!

The bureaucracy itself is a fascinating subject for further discourse. My father once told me with a sense of grim foreboding and after half-heartedly congratulating me for joining the civil service (though I must confess he was relieved that it was the diplomatic service): 'Nothing succeeds like the successor.' I have taken his words to heart as I find it is actually the most useful assessment I have ever received on the state of management science in India — the predecessor is a fool; debunk everything he said and did; start afresh and anew; re-invent the wheel!

It is possible I am being a trifle too harsh as I do perceive in India's young a new attitude, which has begun to affect the older and middle-aged generation of Indians; they talk to their children and realize that the world, as seen through the lens of their children is quite different from the one that they had got used to and even nurtured. The hugely popular Bollywood film *Rang de Basanti* captured this spirit to some extent. The young Indian is no longer willing to shape India through the eyes of his parents, his India would be different and he would mould it in his image. The older generation appears to have largely accepted this attempt at transition and change.

But it is still difficult. There continues to be fairly rampant corruption and huge bureaucratic delays. At lower levels, many would emphatically say that the 'new India' is a myth. I remember once hearing a foreign diplomat, who had just completed his first assignment in India, say in his farewell speech in New Delhi that India makes you weep twice; the first time, when you land in India and tear your hair out of frustration and anguish at so much that is simply not up to the mark and the second time, when you leave India. By then, India has entered your soul and your heart, common people have touched you with the warmth of their smile and their open-hearted hospitality, the sights and smells have now become part of your thinking and your being, and the spirit of India has embraced you without asking for anything in return. Perhaps, that is the story of India and how people relate to this great country and her people.

For those who are impatient for change, it

perhaps bears mentioning that India is a land of 1.3 billion persons. There was a time in 1989 when Europe had not expanded in the way it has today and I would take a map of India and place it on a map of the then-EU. It was amazing for the European parliamentarians to see how the EU was geographically 'swallowed up' by India; even expanded EU does not have the kind of population India has. Indeed, you can drive for miles on end in Australia or Canada or even the US and Europe, and not see a soul or any habitation. Apart from the Thar desert, this is simply not possible anywhere else in India. In terms of population density, the city of Kolkata or Mumbai has more persons than many countries of Europe put together! While it would be fairly normal for our parliamentarians to have around 1.5 to 2 million persons in their constituencies, the average number for parliamentarians in Europe would be around 60,000! The sheer numbers are worth keeping in mind before we are hasty in being judgemental about what is wrong in India. Perhaps, it is not inappropriate to say: hang on! Before you condemn India, think twice. Give India a chance!!

Change is occurring, *albeit* slowly. But it is visible and it is tangible. Indian by choice is today a viable option.

III

It is often difficult to figure out why a book is written and especially in the style that this one is written. I have written this book for my daughter Diya, who is studying in Sydney and who basically feels there is little to call her back to India; perhaps she will now think again. It is also written for my young nephew Varun, who is currently too young to make choices of this magnitude, as also for my

nieces, Mallika and Renee, who live in the US and for my nephews Rahul and Kunal, Abhijit and Siddhartha who are trying to find their feet, either here or where they are. But more importantly, it is written for the nameless person of Indian origin who feels desperately alienated and subscribes to the e-mail reproduced above. Choosing to be Mandy is as difficult as deciding to be Mandeep! Indian by choice is simply not easy.

This book is dedicated to my parents who taught me to give back to India more than I took from her.

I would like to thank my publisher Shobit Arya for the faith he reposed in me. He has been a source of strength. My gratitude goes to Neelabh, without whose help this book in its current graphic format might not have seen the light of day!

My biggest gratitude goes to my wife Deepa. Circumstances and work have forced us to live in two different cities. Neither of us have found the separation easy and we found our own way of coming to terms with it. She plunged into her work and in discovering the city of Kolkata and I sought comfort in writing. It, nevertheless, has been difficult and I know that she has borne the absence with her quiet strength. Her support and her love is what has sustained me and made the writing of this book possible.

For the new and resurgent India, let us be grateful to the younger generation! The future of India lies with them but it is upto us to leave a future they can work with!

Amit Dasgupta
New Delhi; September, 2008